BOOKS BY

RAYMUND FITZSIMONS

Death and the Magician: the Mystery of Houdini   *(1981)*
Edmund Kean: Fire from Heaven   *(1976)*
Garish Lights: an Account of the Public Readings of Dickens   *(1970)*

Death and the Magician

THE MYSTERY OF
HOUDINI

Death and the Magician

THE MYSTERY OF HOUDINI

by

RAYMUND FITZSIMONS

New York ATHENEUM *1981*

Library of Congress Cataloging in Publication Data

FitzSimons, Raymund.
    Death and the magician.

    Bibliography: P.
    Includes index.
    1. Houdini, Harry, 1874-1926. 2. Magicians—
United States—Biography. I. Title.
GV1545.H8F57   1981   793.8′092′4 [B]   80-21071
ISBN 0-689-11122-3

To Lucy

I dedicate this story of a strange and wondrous man, who has haunted my imagination ever since I was nine years old and picked from the shelves of Whitehaven Public Library a book about him. I noticed the book because it was the most tattered volume on the shelves. The pages were dirty, greasy, and thumb-marked. I borrowed the book, reasoning that if so many people had read it there must be something of interest in it . . . there was.

Contents

List of Illustrations

Part One

For all the sleightes and turning of thyne honde
Thou must come nere this dance to understonde;
Nought may avail all thy conclusions,
For Deth shortly, nether on see nor londe,
Is not dyceyved by noon illusions.

Lines addressed by Death to John Rekyll,
Court Magician to King Henry V. From
'The Dance of Death' painted in the
north cloister of Old St Paul's Church,
London, in the reign of Henry VI.

Chapter One

'BEHOLD A MIRACLE'

Right from the start let us call him Houdini.

He was born in Hungary, in Budapest, on 24 March 1874, but for some reason no one has ever satisfactorily explained he always celebrated his birthday on 6 April. He was the son of Jewish parents, Samuel and Cecilia Weiss, who named him Ehrich. His mother said that as a baby he never cried. If he was troubled in any way, she had only to hold him to her heart and the sound of her heart beat soothed him. She worried because he seemed to sleep so little; whenever she bent over him, day or night, his blue-grey eyes were open, looking up at her.

Shortly after his birth, the family sailed to New York and then continued on a long journey inland by rail, canal boat, and lake steamer to the town of Appleton, in the state of Wisconsin. There Samuel became the rabbi at the recently formed synagogue. Samuel was only forty-five years old but he could not adjust to his new life in the bustling mid-West. It was as though the move had drained him of all energy and hope. He was a cultured man, but he made no attempt to learn the English language. Neither did his wife. She was thirteen years his junior and not only loved her ineffectual husband but also revered him. If German was the language he preferred, then she too would speak it. So Houdini grew up speaking German at home, while outside he spoke American, slangy and ungrammatical.

Unlike Samuel, Cecilia was happy in America, as she would have been in any place on earth as long as she was with her husband and her children. Her real world was the home that contained her family, and that family was a large one and still growing. There were the children born in Hungary—Herman, Samuel's son by a previous marriage, Nathan, William, and Houdini. Three more were to be born in America—Theo, Leopold, and Gladys. In addition, Cecilia's mother had come over with them.

As rabbi, Samuel failed to satisfy the Jewish community of Appleton. They found him too old-fashioned, and eventually he was dismissed and replaced by a more progressive man. This caused great hardship to his family, since there was no other work for which he was suited. In 1883 they moved to Milwaukee, but again he could find no work. Herman and Nathan provided the family income. Also Houdini, who at nine years already showed a mature sense of responsibility. He brought in money by selling newspapers and working as a bootblack. Samuel sat at home all day distressed at his inability to support his family. Cecilia comforted him, creating for him the European environment in which he felt most at ease, encouraging him to lose himself in his rabbinical studies.

The home was a happy one, filled with love. Cecilia, tiny, now growing stout, laughing merrily as she went about her household affairs, more than made up for the lamentations of Samuel. And Houdini watched her, always looking for ways to please her, to help her. His father may have found it hard to adjust to a new life in America, but Houdini had a far greater problem; he was never to adapt himself to a separate existence from his mother. He would look at her sewing in her chair, or working in the kitchen, and try to contemplate a world without her. All children have a fear of their parents dying; such fears generally abate as the child grows older, but with Houdini they raged and surged. When his agony became too much for him to bear, he would lay his head against his mother's heart. The strong beat reassured him as it had always done, and as he listened he prayed that his own heart would stop before hers did.

Death visited the family when Houdini was ten years old, taking away his half-brother, Herman, at the age of twenty-two. The house was sad for many months afterwards. Houdini was no longer the only member of the family to brood on death. Samuel, since the loss of his first-born, had thought of little else and had convinced himself that his own end could not be long delayed. On Houdini's twelfth birthday he confided this fear to his son. He had been impressed by the serious sense of purpose shown by the boy, and so he asked him to promise solemnly that as long as he lived he would always take care of his mother. No promise could have been more willingly given or so speedily acted upon. Houdini believed that the time had come to provide for both his parents. Early next morning, while they were still asleep, he left home to seek his fortune in the world. He sent them a postcard to tell them that he was on his way to Texas and would be home in about a year.

The initiative shown by his twelve-year-old son jolted Samuel into making an effort of his own. He went to New York in the hope that the large Jewish population there could support a Hebrew scholar. He was encouraged to start a small school. His family joined him in New York, and Houdini worked his way across the country to be reunited with them. They all settled in a small apartment at 305 East 69th Street.

But Samuel's effort was not sustained. He had been impelled to make the move, but having made it he was again exhausted. All he could do was sit at home and pray, while his children went out to work. Houdini did all kinds of odd jobs and he loved giving his earnings to his mother, knowing he was making her life easier. As he poured the nickels and dimes into her outspread apron, she would laugh and sing while his father raised his hands thankfully to Heaven. In November 1888, when he was fourteen years old, Houdini found a steady job as a neck-tie lining cutter at H. Richter's Sons, and there he discovered magic.

*

Magic as practised in the nineteenth century was chiefly a theatrical entertainment, and among those who had brought its presentation to a high level was Carl Herrmann. Carl had become a magician in Paris in the eighteen-thirties; slim and elegant, he cultivated a satanic look with black moustache and pointed beard.

The implication that he was in league with the devil evoked ancient vibrations in his audiences, for a belief in such a liaison was as old as mankind itself. He took his magic through Europe, performing before kings, queens, and emperors. Magic became a fashionable pursuit among the ruling families, and Carl initiated some members into its mysteries. They showered him with gifts made of gold and precious stones. In 1861, when he visited New York, all these gifts were displayed at Tiffany's, and crowds stared wide-eyed and open-mouthed at the glittering presents from Emperor Franz Joseph of Austria, King Ludwig of Bavaria, the King of Portugal, King Frederick of Denmark, and Queen Isabella of Spain. He returned to Europe, to Vienna, where Baron de Rothschild took private lessons from him and advised him how to invest the vast fortune he had made. As he grew old, he retired to a secluded life, but he was not forgotten by his royal initiates. On his seventieth birthday, Queen Marie Henriette of the Belgians sent him greetings and told him that she had never revealed any of his secrets.

In New York, in 1869, he had introduced his younger brother, Alexander, and designated him as his successor. Alexander styled himself Herrmann the Great and like his brother cultivated the satanic image. Never for a moment, whether onstage or off, did Herrmann the Great cease to be a magician. His everyday actions were touched with wonder. He plucked cab fares out of the air; cigars from the whiskers of his guests; his wine glass vanished after he had emptied it; and the rolls served to him in restaurants were found to contain gold coins or diamond rings. In 1876 he made America his home, but he also toured abroad. Royalty honoured him as they had honoured his brother. In Rio de Janeiro, the Emperor of Brazil attended no fewer than nineteen of his performances, and in Madrid King Alfonso of Spain invited him to his palace.

For years Herrmann the Great had been the leading magician in America, but around the time Houdini and his family settled in New York, a rival had come into the field. He was Harry Kellar, a native-born American. Kellar was not such a virtuoso as Herrmann, nor with his round face and bald head could he cultivate the satanic image. But he introduced little devils into his posters; they perched on his shoulders and whispered in his ears. And he created a wonderful world of illusion in an oriental setting, where beautiful princesses were levitated, cut in half and even vanished completely from the stage. For years he had travelled abroad, not only through Europe but South America and China. These tours were lucrative, for interest in magic was universal and language no barrier. He travelled through India and Egypt, the birthplaces of magic and mystery, and in his publicity he claimed that his oriental marvels were the result of years of original research; that he had seen fakir miracles at the courts of Moham-medan rajahs, and battled through high Himalayan snows to witness levitations in Tibetan lamaseries.

*

Houdini's first excursions into the art of magic were less accom-plished. He practised simple tricks with cards and coins. His interest was shared by another boy at the neck-tie factory, Jacob Hyman. They exchanged tricks and appeared together in amateur concerts. They practised hard and talked of turning professional. Jacob was stagestruck, and to him magic was a means of getting into showbusiness. Of the two, Houdini was by far the more ambitious, but his aims were vague and undefined. He hoped that magic would take him, as it had taken Herrmann and Kellar, to a world of emperors and kings, of travel through exotic lands. Yet he was aware that despite all that the two great magicians had achieved they still remained mere entertainers, and he doubted that such a destiny would ever satisfy him.

Jacob and he also shared an interest in physical fitness. They joined the Pastime Athletic Club, where Houdini proved to be a strong runner and swimmer. He brought to athletics the same dedication he brought to the study of magic. He vowed never to smoke or drink. He was competitive and trained hard. He won many prizes. A photograph of him at this time shows him stripped for running, his shirt festooned with medals and rosettes; stocky and slightly bow-legged, the face finely formed, the expression serious and proud.

At the Pastime Club Houdini and Jacob met Joe Rinn, an older and richer boy, whose father was manager of Smith & McNell's Hotel, one of the largest in New York. Joe knew a lot about magic and had actually seen Herrmann the Great and Kellar. A friendship developed and Houdini and Jacob discussed with him the possibility of becoming professional magicians. Joe did not approve of the idea. To him magic was strictly a hobby; he wanted to become a successful business man, and he advised them to do the same. He reminded them that Herrmann the Great and Kellar were at the top of their profession, the only two in the country playing in legitimate theatres with a full two-hour magic show. Below them was a descending hierarchy of magicians who played in vaudeville, dime museums, right down to beer halls, the rock bottom of show business. And very few got beyond the beer halls and the dime museums.

The two boys listened to Joe with respect; he seemed so knowledgeable and sophisticated. He not only knew a lot about magic, he had also attended spiritualist seances, where people claimed the spirits of the dead came back to earth and talked to the living. Houdini was anxious to know whether this was true and he questioned Joe closely. Joe was dubious. In his opinion, most spiritualist mediums were dishonest magicians who had taken the left hand path, claiming that they possessed supernatural power. In doing this they violated the magicians' code. Honest magicians, such as Herrmann the Great and Kellar, regarded themselves as performing artists who mystified by misdirection and skill. While they cultivated a mysterious aura, they were punctilious in explaining their magic to be purely physical, although they never revealed the secrets of their art. But dishonest magicians claimed supernatural power, and they operated in the shadowy world of spiritualism. Here, as in the world of honest magic, there was a descending hierarchy from those who operated at the highest level of society such as Daniel Dunglas Home, who had practised his art in the great houses of Europe, down to the itinerant medium who went from small town to small town, studying the obituary columns in the local newspaper and reading the gravestones in the cemetery to find information with which to astound his clients.

*

The spiritualist movement, Houdini learned, was a home-grown product, as American as the telephone and the automobile. It had started forty years earlier, in the winter of 1848, when the Fox family moved into a house at Hydesville, near Rochester, N.Y. The family consisted of the father, mother, and two daughters, Margaret aged fifteen and Kate aged twelve. Shortly after they moved in, rappings were heard, noises as if the furniture was being moved around. The parents believed the house to be haunted.

Then Kate asked the ghost to answer when she snapped her fingers; it rapped in reply. Margaret snapped her fingers; the ghost rapped again. The children were delighted; they thought it an exciting game. The mother suggested one rap for 'yes' and two for 'no'. Now the family were able to communicate with the ghost. They learned that it was the spirit of a man, who had been murdered in the house. A neighbour suggested calling out letters of the alphabet, so that the spirit could answer when appropriate. Now words and sentences could be built up, and they learned that the murdered man was buried in the cellar. A search was made, but had to be abandoned because the ground under the cellar was waterlogged.

The rappings came from all parts of the house. The crowds that flocked there were puzzled, for it seemed that none of the family could possibly have caused them. Then the rappings were linked with the children, for when they were taken away to another house the noises followed them.

The affair was arousing national interest so Leah, their elder married sister, began exploiting the girls commercially. In 1850, she brought them to New York as professional mediums. The seances were held in the dark, because the sisters said the spirits preferred it that way. In addition to the rappings, new phenomena occurred—people were caressed by invisible hands, untouched musical instruments played, and the table not only tilted in various directions but even rose from the floor.

All over America mediums began surfacing. To believers this was the time of a new Revelation, a new Pentecost; God manifesting himself through certain chosen people. And at the start it was all so American; even the spirit guides were Red Indians. Some of the faithful found this a little disturbing and even socially unacceptable; they had hardly expected their loved ones to communicate through a savage, no matter how nobly he expressed himself. But when it was pointed out that no other race in America believed in spirits so fervently as the Red Indians, and that this was why they occupied such commanding positions as intermediaries between the living and the dead, then everyone was happy.

Communication methods were improving all the time. Spirits not only rapped but wrote their messages on slates and, most wonderful of all, sometimes came in person to deliver their messages, taking on corporeal forms and allowing themselves to be touched.

The movement spread rapidly to Britain and Europe, where it was embraced by thousands who sincerely believed that God was allowing communication with spirits of the dead. But right from the start the claims of the movement were clouded by the many crazy and fraudulent people who had got in on the game. Dishonest mediums abounded.

All kinds of marvellous manifestations were reported, but the Fox sisters reigned supreme as the first, the purest source. Then, in 1851, they were investigated by three professors from the Buffalo School of Medicine, who gave the opinion that the rappings were made by the sisters dislocating and relocating their knee or toe joints. This report was widely accepted, and many outsiders believed that the damage done to the sisters' reputation would cause the movement to wither and die. But the movement continued to flourish, for those who believed continued to believe. Their faith even survived the confession of one of the sisters that they had indeed cheated.

This confession occurred thirty-seven years later, in the autumn of 1888, when the sisters were in their fifties. Both were in distressed circumstances and both had taken to drink. Margaret confessed that the rappings had been made with their toe joints, and she gave a public demonstration. Newspaper headlines announced that this was the death-blow to spiritualism. But inside the movement the faithful went on believing, granting that on some occasions the sisters might have cheated, but only because their psychic power, wayward and uncontrollable, had temporarily deserted them.

The reaction of the spiritualists to the report of the Buffalo professors and the confession of Margaret Fox demonstrated clearly where the strength of the movement lay. The faithful believed that they had got hold of a fundamental truth in the proven fact that man survives death and can communicate with the living. No matter how loudly sceptics shouted and materialists denied, no matter how scientifically their claims were investigated and dismissed, no matter how many fraudulent mediums were exposed, the spiritualists continued to believe, for their conviction once gained was unshakeable. In any case, Margaret later retracted her confession, stating that she had only made it because she was desperate for money and the New York *World* had offered her fifteen hundred dollars. This retraction boosted the movement. In New York and in every city and town throughout America mediums prospered. Spiritualism, like the American economy, was booming.

*

And it was still booming two years later, when early in 1891, Houdini persuaded Joe Rinn to take him to a seance in New York. Joe took him to the house of Mrs Minnie Williams on Forty-sixth Street. At one dollar per person Houdini thought the admission fee was steep. About forty people were present and he remarked to Joe that there must be plenty of money in the game. Joe whispered that there had to be when she needed to employ bodyguards, and he indicated two very tough looking characters named Bug Macdonald and Jack Thompson. Minnie Williams took her place in a heavily curtained cabinet and appeared to go into a trance. Houdini noticed that at all times she was closely protected by her two gorillas. The curtains of the cabinet were drawn close by

Thompson, who then turned off the light. The room was not completely dark, but it was difficult for anyone in the gathering to distinguish clearly the features of his neighbour.

Thompson led them in a hymn, 'Nearer My God to Thee', then figures began to emerge from the cabinet, sometimes one, sometimes two. If Houdini had been hoping to recognise among them the spirit of his half-brother, Herman, he was disappointed, but the figures were recognised by some of those present as spirits of loved ones who had passed on. The room was now filled with the sounds of grief, of weeping, sighs, and frenzied moans. The spirits, when leaving, consoled the heart-broken, saying in a hoarse voice, 'Gawd bless you.' The floor creaked when they walked, so Houdini reckoned that they were pretty solidly built.

Afterwards, outside, he expressed his amazement that people could be fooled by so obvious a fake. Joe reminded him of Barnum's phrase about a sucker being born every minute. Houdini thought about this and concluded that on the level of parting fools from their money Minnie Williams was perhaps to be admired. Yet at the same time he felt disturbed as he remembered that not everything at the seance had been a fake; the sounds of grief had been genuine beyond all doubt.

Some weeks later Joe showed him a recently published book called *The Revelations of a Spirit Medium*, which exposed nearly every trick used to produced so-called spirit phenomena. Of all the secrets in the book, the one that most fascinated Houdini was the revelation that a person while securely bound with ropes could release himself and get back into his bonds. It was the custom of some mediums to suggest to the sitters that they tie them to a chair. This was to give an assurance to those present that it was impossible for the medium to have any part in the production of the spirit phenomena. The book gave explicit directions on how the rope tie was manipulated. Houdini practised the trick with Jacob; they tied each other up and soon became as expert as any medium.

They went on to study the technique of other rope ties. They learned that it was impossible to tie a man securely with one long length of rope if the tying began at one end and finished at the other, for by expanding the chest or hunching the shoulders slack could be obtained. They also learned that the more spectacular the tie the easier the escape. A man could be lashed to a ladder or spreadeagled on a wheel, yet by straining on the ropes he could release one hand. They discovered that the releasing of one hand was the great secret of escaping from ropes, for then knot after knot could be untied.

They were still weighing up their chances of succeeding as professional magicians and their new found skill with rope ties gave them more confidence. But Houdini still hesitated; he was not yet convinced that magic could take him where he wanted to go. Then in that same year, 1891, he read a book, and any remaining doubts he had were finally resolved. The book was the memoirs of Jean-Eugène Robert-Houdin, who styled himself Ambassador, Author, and Conjuror.

*

Robert-Houdin had begun his series of 'Soirées Fantastiques', in Paris, in 1845, at a theatre in the old Palais Royal. It was a tiny theatre, high-priced and fashionable, holding no more than two hundred people. The stage was designed as a white and gold salon in the style of Louis XV, with crystal chandeliers and golden candelabra. And on that elegant stage the equally elegant Robert-Houdin performed his wonders.

From one ordinary wine bottle he poured any variety of drink requested by members of the audience. Servants passed among them with trays of brimming glasses filled with the finest liqueurs and vintages, all poured from the same bottle. Glass after glass was filled in an inexhaustible stream. An orange tree grew and blossomed on the stage. At a wave of his wand, the blossoms were transformed into delicious oranges, which he plucked and tossed among the audience. From a thin portfolio he produced numerous bulky articles, including a cage of birds, copper pans, some filled with water, some with fire, and, finally, a small boy, his own son. He blindfolded his son, who then described any object shown by the audience to his father. The boy identified not only watches and card cases, but the inscriptions inside their lids; not only coins, but their date and country of origin. Robert-Houdin then levitated his son high above the stage.

All these tricks and many more Robert-Houdin claimed to have invented. As Houdini read on, he began to realise that Herrmann the Great and Kellar were not innovators and masters in their own right, as he had supposed them to be, but mere imitators, or at best disciples of Robert-Houdin, their tricks but variations of his. Here in this book it was all set down, the master of magic revealing himself.

And most marvellous of all, Robert-Houdin's reputation was not confined to the narrow world of entertainment. His country, in its hour of need, sent for him. In 1856, in Algeria, the Marabouts, a band of wonder-working, religious fanatics, were urging the tribes to rise up and overthrow the French. In Paris, the government asked Robert-Houdin to go to Algeria and counteract the influence of the Marabouts by an exhibition of his magic. So he performed before the assembled leaders of all the tribes. His magic astounded them and they believed his powers to be supernatural. They took council among themselves and concluded that the magic of the Marabouts could not be compared to the magic of the French. Peace was restored and Robert-Houdin returned in triumph to Paris.

When Houdini put down the book, he knew that the course of his life had been decided. He would become a professional magician, and through his magic, like Robert-Houdin, he would play a part in world affairs. From that moment on, Robert-Houdin became his hero and that book his gospel. He wished that the magician was still alive so that he could make a pilgrimage to his home at St Gervais. There he would approach the locked entrance gates, and rap on them with the grotesque demon's head which formed the knocker. He would watch as the great gates swung silently open of their own accord, and then he would walk up the long drive and into the house of magic, through trap-doors, descending floors and sliding panels, until he found himself in the presence of the great magician, before whom he would bow his head or even kneel in homage.

*

And so at the age of seventeen he became a professional magician, with Jacob as his partner. A name was needed for their act. Houdini had been talking constantly of Houdin, as he called Robert-Houdin, not realising that he was using only the second part of a hyphenated surname. Jacob had his own mistaken idea that adding 'i' to a name was the European manner for meaning 'like'. He suggested that they call themselves the Houdini Brothers, and this became their name.

Old Samuel was unhappy about his son's decision to become a professional magician; it seemed to him that the most sensible of his children had lost his head. But Cecilia was more tolerant, while Theo, Houdini's younger brother, was filled with admiration and envy. When Joe Rinn heard the news, he advised Houdini to get a good reference from his employers at the neck-tie factory, because in all probability he would need it when he failed as a magician.

And from the start failure seemed inevitable. They played in beer halls, the only dates they could get. Beer halls were not at all like Robert-Houdin's elegant little theatre in the Palais Royal. These were rough, tough, men-only places. The crowded tables were close together, with aisles almost too narrow for the waiters to squeeze themselves along. The air was thick with tobacco smoke and the fumes of alcohol, which made the two clean-living boys gasp and choke. The noise was deafening. The drunken rabble might quieten for a sentimental ballad or a comedian frankly blue, but all other performers had to fight against the hubbub, and the conditions were especially hard for a novelty act featuring two nervous young magicians.

The Houdini Brothers did a fifteen minute act of small magic culminating in a trunk substitution trick. They had purchased the trick from a broken-down magician; it was a wooden trunk with a secret panel which opened inwards. The trunk could be locked and roped, yet a person could escape from inside without disturbing either restraint. The trick had been invented twenty-five years previously by the British magician, John Nevil Maskelyne. He would be locked inside the trunk, which was then lashed with rope and placed behind a screen. He would then appear from behind the screen. The screen would be removed, and there was the trunk still locked and roped.

Houdini had refined the trick. He invited a committee from the audience to come onto the stage, where they bound his hands behind his back. There were always plenty of sailors in the beer hall willing to do this, and all the other roping and tying. He was placed in a sack and the top of the sack was not only tied but also sealed. He was put inside the trunk, which was then locked and lashed with ropes. A cabinet with a metal-pipe frame, curtained with dark blue velvet, was lifted forward to enclose the trunk. Jacob went into the cabinet, but when the curtains were drawn aside it was Houdini who stepped forward. Jacob had vanished, and there stood the trunk locked and roped. The committee un-roped the trunk, unlocked it and then broke the seal and untied the rope on the sack. There inside was Jacob, his hands securely tied behind his back as Houdini's had been. The audience were baffled, for the time spent inside the cabinet had not been long enough for the substitution to have been achieved by any normal means. Houdini named the trick 'Metamorphosis'.

Metamorphosis was a good trick. The audience had been mis-directed into believing that Houdini was lying bound inside the tied and sealed sack when the curtains of the cabinet closed round the locked trunk. But as soon as he had been placed in the sack he had begun releasing his hands, so that by the time the sack was tied they were free and ready, waiting for the moment the lid was locked so that he could open the bottom of the sack by slitting the seam. By the time the curtains of the cabinet closed round the trunk he was out of the sack, poised to release the secret panel and so escape. The instant Jacob entered the trunk, Houdini flung back the curtains and revealed himself. Jacob was now working the reverse procedure inside the trunk, and by the time this had been unroped and unlocked he was a prisoner inside a tied sack, to be revealed bound in exactly the same manner Houdini had been. He was in a sitting position when the neck of the sack was untied. He did not move from that position, so no one suspected that the bottom of the sack, which they could not see, had been cut.

Metamorphosis relied for its effect on speed and Houdini wanted it done faster and faster; but Jacob could not work inside the trunk so quickly as Houdini. He tried hard to increase his speed, but it was becoming obvious that he would always be the slower of the two. In addition, they were having disagreements over other aspects of the act. After four months the partnership broke up. Jacob renounced magic, changed his name to Jack Hayman, and made his way in showbusiness as a song and dance man.

Houdini needed a new partner. He approached his brother Theo and Theo was delighted to accept. To Samuel the thought that two of his sons were now magicians was incomprehensible. He was failing fast, and in his distress it was to Houdini, of all his children, that he turned. He recognised in his fine-featured son a boy of responsibility, of high moral purpose; a boy who could be a great lawyer or doctor, one to whom people with problems would always turn, as he was turning now; a boy who should not be wasting his life escaping from a trunk. The world had become too puzzling for Samuel. In the early autumn of 1892 he made Houdini repeat solemnly the promise of his twelfth birthday to look after his mother. A few weeks later he died. 'Weiss, Weiss,' Cecilia wailed, 'you have left me with your children.'

*

The shadow of his father's death accompanied Houdini as he and Theo wandered the country from one beer hall to the next. They travelled far and unsuccessfully. On stage the Houdini Brothers made an odd looking pair. Theo was always smartly dressed, which is why everyone called him Dash, while Houdini's suits were rumpled and stained, for no man cared less about dress. Metamorphosis was still the main trick. Dash was a shade faster than Jacob, but his speed was still not fast enough for Houdini. To work out which routine was the quicker they took turns at being the one who escaped. But one night Dash was unable to get out of the trunk and the performance ended disastrously. After this it was always Houdini who made the escape.

In 1893 they were drawn to Chicago by the World's Columbian Exposition. For some years past there had been much discussion in the press and in Congress as to how the four hundredth anniversary of Christopher Columbus's discovery of America in 1492 should be commemorated. It was finally decided that an international exhibition should form the centrepiece of the celebrations, but there were so many arguments over its location that when Chicago was finally chosen time had run out. Acting, however, on the motto of better late than never, the project had been moved forward to 1893. One of the chief attractions of the Exposition was the Midway Plaisance, where visitors could see sideshows from all over the world. Here puritanical America was introduced to the erotic belly dancing of Egyptian dancing girls; an art form that not only proved popular but also influential, leading to a national craze for the hootchy-kootchy and starting a tradition of girlie sideshows.

The Midway attracted entertainers and tricksters from all over America. Minnie Williams was there. Assisted by her two gorillas, she honoured the celebrations by bringing back on earth not the spirits of any Tom, Dick, or Harry, but by communing loftily with such great souls as Aristotle, Jesus Christ, and Henry Ward Beecher. The Houdini Brothers appeared on the Midway, and it was there that Houdini saw a performer escape from a pair of handcuffs.

The Handcuff Act was a simple trick. The handcuffs were locked on the performer and a large handkerchief thrown over them. Under the cover of this, he opened the cuffs with a duplicate key. In those days most handcuffs of the same make and model opened with the same key, so all the performer had to do was to get the keys of all the makes in current use. This fact, of course, was unknown to the audience, who watched intrigued as the performer struggled desperately to free himself. Houdini practised the trick over and over again. The Handcuff Act fascinated him. He found that whenever the handcuffs were snapped on his wrists he experienced a profound stirring of the imagination. He began to think how wonderful and mystifying it would be if he could discard the duplicate keys and devise some other method of escape. He had already acquired the skill of escaping from rope ties but he knew that this could not be compared with the ability to break free of locked handcuffs and other metal restraints.

At first he performed the trick in the same way as other magicians, and while in Chicago he became so proficient that he was invited to appear without Dash at Kohl and Middleton's Dime Museum. This was a move in the right direction, for while dime museums were by no means places of high class entertainment they were a step above beer halls. Unlike those men-only dives the audience was mixed and blue material banned. The better ones, such as Kohl and Middleton's, liked to regard themselves as educational institutions and divided their interiors into two sections, one for the exhibition of freaks and curios, and the other for variety shows. The exhibition room at Kohl and Middleton's housed at various times, for the edification of the American public, midgets, giants, fat ladies, bird girls, and dog-faced boys, while in the variety hall jugglers, magicians, puppeteers and clog dancers provided light relief from these thought-provoking exhibits. Houdini was billed as 'Handcuff King and Escape Artist'. The work was hard; never less than five shows a day, rising to seventeen or even twenty at weekends and holidays. The pay was twelve dollars a week.

For both Houdini and Dash the stay in Chicago was profitable, but later in the year they were back in New York, back again to the beer halls. The Handcuff Act had been added to the repertoire, but Metamorphosis was still their main attraction. Houdini was far from satisfied with the speed of the exchange, but he realised that Dash could go no faster.

In the summer of 1894 they got a booking at Coney Island and among the many attractions at that blaring, raucous pleasure-ground was a genteel act called 'The Floral Sisters, Neat Song and Dance Artists'. Dash dated one of the sisters and then introduced her to Houdini. She was a sweet faced, childlike brunette, tiny and slightly built. Her name was Wilhelmina Beatrice Rahmer, Bess for short; the daughter of German immigrants. Houdini fell in love with her at first sight. Within a fortnight they were married. He was twenty, she was eighteen. It was a civil ceremony. She was a Catholic, he was a Jew. The marriage caused the break-up of the Houdini Brothers, for Houdini intended to take Bess into the act. It was the obvious thing to do; a husband and wife team could pool their wages and save on expenses.

The break-up was a friendly one, and after the last show they did together Houdini asked Dash and Bess to come for a walk with him. It was a night Bess was never to forget; her earliest intimation that the young magician she had married could not be measured by the standards of ordinary men. They stopped at a lonely bridge over swift dark water. A crescent moon was moving in and out of heavy clouds. They stood silently waiting. The bells began to chime midnight and Houdini clasped all their hands together and held them high to heaven. He asked them to swear that they would both be true to him and never betray him in any way. Bess was startled by his intensity. After they had sworn he seemed relieved and he told them that he knew they would always keep that sacred oath.

*

Houdini took his wife home to meet his mother and the rest of his family. Cecilia received Bess kindly and the young couple made their home in the crowded apartment. Their bedroom was the only place they could be alone, and there Houdini showed Bess his magic. Coins and cards vanished from his fingertips. The name of a person she was thinking about appeared in flaming letters on his bared arm. This frightened her, but he soothed her, telling her that it was only a trick. Then he showed her another trick, which he said he had learned from a Hindu conjuror in Chicago. He swallowed a length of thread and then a handful of needles. She knew he had swallowed them, for he opened his mouth and it was empty. Then the end of the thread appeared between his lips. He beckoned to her to take hold of it. She took it gingerly between her finger and thumb. He began stepping slowly backwards and from his mouth came the needles, all threaded, one after the other at regular intervals, until a full two dozen hung on the line stretched between them. She could only look at him, amazed.

Then he told her all his dreams; how he would have his own full two-hour show of magic and play in the finest theatres throughout the world; how kings and emperors would honour him. He told her of the vast sums of money a master magician could make; how Herrmann the Great lived in a mansion on Long Island, sailed in a glittering yacht and travelled in his own luxurious private railway car. He told her that he would become the greatest magician in the world, perhaps the greatest of all time. Then when his reputation was made, he would step onto the wider stage of the world and perform some outstanding service to humanity.

She listened enthralled to her serious young husband as he poured out these proud hopes. He was so confident, so spellbinding that the fact that his lofty ambitions were voiced in ungrammatical English did not strike her as incongruous even when he went on to tell her of the scholarly books he intended to write. For in Bess he had found the perfect wife, and he gained from her in those early days what he was to enjoy throughout his life—her utter devotion and her complete identification with all his hopes.

And she soon learned how hard he was prepared to work to achieve his ambitions. His energy was prodigious. He slept no more than five hours a night. The rest of the time was spent exercising his body, practising with ropes and handcuffs, playing with coins and cards to keep his fingers supple. In the first days of their marriage he instructed her in the part she would play in the act, emphasising the importance of speed in Metamorphosis. Hour after hour they practised in the bedroom. She fitted into the trunk better than Dash had done; she was only half his size.

Soon 'The Houdinis', as they called themselves, were ready for the beer halls and dime museums. They had rigged themselves out in new costumes. Bess in her brief but decorous top and ill-fitting tights looked like a nervous schoolgirl dressed up for a Christmas concert. Houdini wore evening dress with a flower in his buttonhole, but the suit was creased and far too big for his stocky body. Yet this did not detract from his dignity. The force of his presence came over the footlights. His expression was grave, and to many people in the audience his powerful head, wide brow and aquiline nose suggested a bust of a Roman consul or general.

When the curtained cabinet had been lifted forward to enclose the trunk, Bess addressed the audience. 'When I clap my hands three times,' she said, 'behold a miracle!' She darted into the cabinet and three claps were heard. The claps were made by Houdini, already out of the trunk. Then he drew back the curtain. Behind him was the trunk still locked and roped. Bess had disappeared. And this had happened within three seconds.

The audience murmured wonderingly. They asked themselves if what they had witnessed had really happened. Yet it had happened. Two people bound and sealed had been transported through space, through sacks and strong nailed boards at a speed that outstripped the rapidity of thought. This was the effect Houdini had worked to achieve. His technique had transcended physical barriers to produce what was perhaps truly a miracle.

Chapter Two

NAKED AND BOUND IN CHAINS

The Houdinis travelled the country with Metamorphosis, and the success of the trick enabled them to get bookings in dime museums rather than beer halls. The reputation of the trick spread throughout the entertainment world, and in January 1895 Houdini received an offer to play at Tony Pastor's vaudeville theatre in New York. He believed that the breakthrough had come at last. Vaudeville was in an entirely different league from beer halls and dime museums; it was the great American entertainment, as brassy and assured as America itself. And Tony Pastor was king of vaudeville. He had started it fourteen years previously, on 24 October 1881, when he opened his Fourteenth Street Theatre. There he put on shows three times a day, with a bill of comedians, song and dance teams, and speciality acts. These were clean shows, family shows; there was no smut in vaudeville. To top the bill in vaudeville with a fifteen to thirty minute act was the ultimate ambition of most magicians, for only a Herrmann or a Kellar, the very greatest, could rise above it and put on a full two-hour show in legitimate theatres.

Joe Rinn received a letter from Houdini expressing his joy at the booking. Joe went hopefully to the opening performance, but his heart sank when he saw the Houdinis were the opening act, the worst place on the bill. Even the effect of Metamorphosis was lost on an unsettled audience occupied with finding their seats or divesting themselves of overcoats. Tony Pastor found the act no more than satisfactory and did not extend the booking beyond the week.

Houdini and Bess were now in New York, out of work, but for

B

Houdini there were compensations. He was back with his mother, his other sweetheart, as he called her, and he also saw a lot of Joe Rinn. Joe was well on his way to achieving his ambition to become a successful businessman, and he was also making a reputation for himself as a serious investigator of psychic phenomena. He told Houdini that his great hope was to find a genuine medium, preferably one who could materialise spirits. He had attended innumerable seances, but so far had found no one. Houdini told him he was wasting his time, as all mediums were fakes.

Between scattered engagements, Houdini continued to study the art of magic. He was always increasing his repertoire and now he added 'Second Sight' to his skills. The Second Sight mystery was one of the most baffling in magic. Robert-Houdin claimed to have invented it. His son, though blindfolded, was able to identify any object presented by the audience. Most people believed the boy to be especially gifted, but Robert Heller, a young magician who witnessed the exhibition, thought otherwise. He was convinced that Robert-Houdin, while addressing his son, was using an elaborate word code to pass on the character of the object displayed. Heller was a magician with great style; his performances were noted for their wit and elegance. He was a gifted concert pianist and his evening of magic and music was always in demand in the salons of the rich. After much practice he perfected a Second Sight routine that was far more sensational than Robert-Houdin's.

Heller classified every variety of object into sets, and devised a word code that embraced every one of them. This he simplified, so that one question with a word or two added could elicit a correct answer for ten different objects. The most difficult part of the business was mastering the code, but once this was done the rest was comparatively easy. He continued to improve his routine by inventing a silent code to be used in conjunction with the verbal one. By natural movements of his body he conveyed secret signals to a confederate, who telegraphed them by means of an electrical device to the clairvoyant sitting blindfolded in the chair. The performance was so baffling, so uncanny, that many people believed it must be supernatural.

Houdini's Second Sight routine was not so sophisticated. His code was comprised of spoken words and sometimes body movements which could be spotted through a trick blindfold. Bess and he practised every day in their bedroom at his mother's apartment. They practised until he was satisfied that the routine was perfect enough to go into the act. And he continued to be obsessed by the idea of escaping from metal restraints. He visited pawnshops and scrap yards, buying up all the handcuffs he could find. He took the cuffs apart and put them together again, working out ways of opening them without using a key, ways he could practise out of sight of the audience, in the secrecy of his curtained cabinet.

He found that some makes could be opened with a sharp blow, by striking the part of the cuff between the hinge and the keyhole on the heel of the shoe or against the floor. To prevent noise, a piece of lead could be sewn in the trousers above the knee, bent to the shape of the leg, so that it would not be noticeable. When the handcuff was struck against the leg, the fabric of the trousers deadened the sound. Moreover, because the bolt shot out from under the lock, he would be able to let members of the audience place sealing wax over the lock, then he would emerge from the cabinet with the cuffs still locked and the seal intact. He hoped that this would create a most mysterious effect.

But some makes could not be opened so easily. There was the plug lock, so called because after locking the cuffs a small steel plug was inserted in the circular keyhole. The key had two teeth at one end to unscrew the plug. Then the other end was inserted in the keyhole to open the lock. This was a difficult lock to master, but eventually he devised a pick with a wooden cogwheel which revolved when rolled against the floor of the cabinet and so unscrewed the plug.

He was still pursuing his studies in April, when Bess and he joined the Welsh Brothers' Circus on a contract for twenty-six weeks. The money was poor; their joint wage was twenty-five dollars a week plus food. But after scratching around for odd engagements, six months solid work seemed an attractive prospect. The Welsh Brothers' 'Mighty Cavalcade and Giant Attraction' was a small travelling circus without animals. The Houdinis joined it in Lancaster, Pennsylvania and went on to tour small rural towns in the east. The main features of their act were Metamorphosis, Second Sight and the Handcuff Escape. Houdini also performed several conjuring tricks, of which the most mysterious was the Needle Trick, which he had learned from the Hindu conjurer in Chicago.

In this trick he produced about fifty needles and ten yards of thread and invited a committee from the audience to examine the inside of his mouth to see if he had anything hidden there. They found nothing. Then he put the needles and thread in his mouth and appeared to swallow them. After a few seconds, he brought the needles out of his mouth all threaded. It was a baffling trick. No matter how thoroughly a committee searched his mouth they always failed to find there a bundle of needles already threaded. Wherever Houdini had hidden them—in his gullet, under his tongue, or up the nose passage at the back of his throat—no one ever succeeded in finding them.

The Needle Trick was always received with murmurs of wonder, as were Metamorphosis and Second Sight. But the Handcuff Escape aroused little interest, the audience assuming that he used duplicate keys or doctored cuffs. He was beginning to realise that the Handcuff Escape had been so widely practised by so many inept performers that it had now become a derisory exhibition. Yet he continued to persevere with it for escaping from metal restraints had for him a significance he could not explain.

The season with the circus ended and there was no further work for the Houdinis. They could always go back to the beer halls and the dime museums, but Houdini saw no future in that. Bess and he had some money. They had lived thriftily with the circus, spending almost nothing. Each week he had sent half their wage to his mother, the rest he had saved. He now used these savings to buy an interest in a run-down burlesque show called 'The American Gaiety Girls', a company of eight girls and six men. Burlesque had not yet acquired its disreputable name, although the emphasis was already on the chorus girls and the comedians made frequent references to their anatomy.

In the autumn of 1895, 'The American Gaiety Girls' began a

tour of small eastern towns. Houdini was continuing to increase his knowledge of handcuffs, and during the tour he could sometimes, with confidence, visit the police at the local police station and escape from their cuffs, alone in an adjoining room. This was usually reported in the local paper, giving publicity to the show. Yet onstage the Handcuff Escape still failed to impress. He invited members of the audience to inspect the handcuffs, to lock and unlock them as often as they wished, to examine them closely to see whether they were doctored. Then he would escape from the cuffs in the secrecy of his cabinet and emerge holding them dramatically above his head. But the audience were sceptical that there was anything at all mysterious about this. If, as he claimed, the cuffs were not doctored and he did not use duplicate keys, then they assumed that he had trained the muscles of his hands to contract so that the cuffs slipped over them.

To prove this was not so, he extended his repertoire to include ratchet handcuffs which could not be slipped as they could be adjusted to any degree of tightness on the wrist, and other makes which were so designed that the more the prisoner struggled the tighter the cuffs closed on him. To open these he devised picks shaped like nails, pins, or prongs, which could be hammered lightly into the floor of the cabinet or hidden in its draperies. But no matter how difficult the handcuff might be, the escape failed to grip the audience. Yet he continued to persevere with the act, for he was convinced that if escaping from handcuffs had a fascination for him then somehow, someday, he would make it equally fascinating for an audience.

*

The Handcuff Escape was a failure and other parts of the show were doing no better, with the result that in the spring of 1896 'The American Gaiety Girls' folded at Woonsacket, Long Island. The Houdinis were again out of work and it was only desperation that made them sign up with Marco the Magician for a tour of the Canadian Maritime Provinces. Marco was the stage name of Edward J. Dooley, of Connecticut. By profession he was a church organist and choir master, but he was also a part-time magician with unfortunate delusions of grandeur. For years he had saved for this show, a full evening of magic patterned after that of Herrmann the Great. He called it his 'Farewell Tour', although he had made no previous ones, and to Houdini's chagrin he claimed vicarious credit for Metamorphosis and the Handcuff Escape by announcing that all his strenuous feats would be performed by 'his daughter and son-in-law, Bessie and Harry Houdini'. Marco's show was an ill-fated venture doomed from the start. It opened and closed in Halifax, Nova Scotia. In lieu of wages, he handed over the show to 'his daughter and son-in-law' and returned to his organ and his choir. Houdini took the show to various towns, but with little success.

This was a miserable time for him, not merely because of the failure of the show but also because here, in an unfamiliar country, away from his mother, he was haunted more than ever by thoughts of her death. He could not bear the prospect of a world without her; he believed that in such a world he would surely go out of his mind. This made him morbidly curious about the condition of the insane, and while at St John, New Brunswick, he visited the lunatic asylum. He was shown round by Dr Steeves, the director. During the tour they stopped outside a heavily bolted door with a narrow grille. Houdini looked through the grille and saw a violent patient, in a padded cell, trying to free himself from a strait-jacket.

Houdini had never seen this type of restraint before. It was an upper garment made of strong brown canvas, but the opening was not at the front but at the back, where it was fastened with leather straps and metal buckles. The patient could not possibly unfasten these, since his arms were folded across his chest, and encased in sleeves so long that they met at the back of the body, one overlapping the other. Moreover, these sleeves were not open at the end but closed, and attached to them were straps and buckles, which again fastened at the back of the body.

Houdini watched amazed as the patient flung himself against the walls and rolled on the floor in his frantic effort to remove the terrible restraint. Dr Steeves remarked that only a madman would make such an attempt. The more the patient struggled the tighter the strait-jacket encircled him, and eventually he lay exhausted on the floor, panting and grunting. That night Houdini tossed restlessly in bed. Whenever he dropped off to sleep, he dreamed of strait-jackets, lunatics, and padded cells.

The next morning he returned to the asylum and begged Dr Steeves to give him an old strait-jacket. The doctor gave him one and Houdini went straight back to his room and began to practise with it. To Bess it must have seemed that he had indeed gone mad. He made her bind him in the heavy garment. Her fingers ached from fastening the cruel buckles. Then she watched his effort to escape. Hour after hour the agonising struggle went on until, like the lunatic, he lay exhausted on the floor. Bess released him and the next day he tried again. Day after day he struggled on, his body bruised and aching, his fingers raw and bleeding. Then on the seventh day he succeeded. By sheer strength and persistent straining, he brought his enclosed arms in front of his body. Then he undid the buckles of the sleeve straps with his teeth. His arms were still enclosed, but reaching behind he unfastened the rest of the buckles through the canvas. This was painfully difficult, but practice with rope ties had made his fingers strong. As he removed the strait-jacket and dropped it to the floor, a sensation of freedom swept over him, such as he had never before experienced. It was as though he had shed not the strait-jacket but some of the fears that troubled him.

He introduced the escape into Marco's show, releasing himself behind the curtains of his cabinet. He emerged dishevelled, perspiring, and threw down the strait-jacket triumphantly. But his exhilaration was not shared by the audience. They could not believe that a stage performer would go to such extremes in order to escape, and they concluded that he must be faking. And it must have occurred to Houdini that his performance was far removed from the art of magic, an art which combined skill with elegance. What he had done was no more than an exhibition of brute strength. This was not the way of his hero, Robert-Houdin, or of Herrmann the Great or Kellar. Their most energetic physical motion was no more than the gracious waving of their wand; they would never have taken their final bow in torn clothes, panting for breath.

Herrmann the Great was touring the United States at the time. He was still the finest magician in America, but he now paid Kellar the honour of acknowledging him as his most serious rival. He competed openly with him by adding large-scale illusions to his show, knowing these to be Kellar's chief attraction. In his illusions Herrmann featured his beautiful wife, Adelaide. In 'Cremation' she was burned alive, and in 'After the Ball' she vanished as she stood admiring herself before a large mirror. Kellar countered these with 'Astarte, Maid of the Moon', in which a houri was not only levitated but turned slowly and gracefully head over heels in the air.

Houdini had followed all these developments closely, and on his return to the States he hoped to meet Herrmann the Great. He wanted to ask him a question, a question that always came into his mind after he had performed Metamorphosis. Was it just the relentless application of technique which produced a seemingly magic effect; or could it be that technique when so perfected could unleash at the critical moment some psychic force which caused an effect that was truly magic? But the question was not to be put.

After playing the Lyceum in Rochester, Herrmann the Great drove in his four horse carriage to the railroad depot and boarded his private car, which had cost forty thousand dollars and once belonged to Lily Langtry. Attached to this were the baggage cars carrying his equipment, and a special car for the coach and horses. He was off to Bradford, Pennsylvania, where he was to open the following night. But on the morning of 17 December, 1896, as he sat in his luxurious compartment, smoking one cigarette after the other, his satanic features set in their customary expression of brooding contemplation, Death came for him.

*

Meanwhile Houdini, weak and trembling from seasickness, landed at Boston from Canada. He eventually reached New York, tired, hungry, and penniless. After five years as a professional magician, he was back where he started. It seemed to him that for those long years he had been going in the wrong direction. He had no immediate intention of abandoning magic, but he felt the need to approach it in a different way. But somehow he had a living to make. Joe Rinn wanted to help him financially, but Houdini would not allow this. Bess and he were living rent-free with his mother, but this did not trouble him; they had always sent her half their money when working and the apartment was their home as well as hers. He was so glad to be with her again. He had always hated touring, because this took him away from her, and now he looked round for work that would keep him in New York.

He began exploring the business side of magic. He saw no further need for the tricks he had used in his act, so he tried to sell them. He advertised Metamorphosis, the Needle Trick and his Second Sight routine, but there were no takers. He opened a correspondence course in the art of magic, but he enrolled very few pupils. He also acted as agent for Roterberg, the Chicago manufacturer of magical equipment. Some of the tricks in the catalogue were used by fake mediums in spiritualist seances—how to fold papers in darkened rooms; how to cause an accordion to play even though the instrument was tied up and sealed; and how to materialise spirit forms. As far as Roterberg, or any other manufacturer of magical equipment was concerned, all these were merely tricks; the use to which they were put was not their affair. The tricks were used by professional and amateur magicians. If, at the same time, the manufacturers were cashing in on the craze for spiritualism, then why not? They reasoned that if there were people so deluded as to believe these tricks to be supernatural manifestations, then they deserved to be taken for a ride. So they cheerfully sold slate writing secrets, table lifting methods, or even complete large or economy sized kits of assorted dark room phenomena.

This view was shared by Houdini. He advertised his own course for anyone thinking of setting up as a medium. He promised to instruct them thoroughly, either personally or by mail, in rope-tying, clairvoyance, and the conjuring up of materialised spirits. But none of his business ventures was successful and in the autumn of 1897, he was on the road again; just Bess and he with the same old act, the one he could not even sell. It was a disastrous tour. In Milwaukee they were swindled out of their wages, and the winter found them stranded in St Louis. By December, tired of the uncertainty of week to week engagements, they accepted an offer from a mid-western medicine show of fifteen weeks at twenty-five dollars a week. They joined 'The California Concert Company' at Garnett, Kansas.

Medicine shows were the outlet for patent medicines in the scattered towns in the wide open spaces of America. These medicines could be big business. Concoctions such as Lydia Pinkham's Compound and Radom's Microbe Killer sold millions of bottles a year. The California Concert Company was run by 'Doctor' Hill. With his flowing beard and long brown hair he looked more distinguished than many a legitimate medical man. The company consisted of his partner, 'Doctor' Pratt, and a few variety acts. During the day Doc Hill sold his remedies at street corners, attracting a crowd with organ music and song. Then his silvery tongue spoke eloquently of the almost miraculous properties of his products, relating how these had cured cases of which the finest medical minds in the world had despaired. As he spoke, members of the company went among the crowd, selling the bottles. He finished by inviting everybody to come that evening to an entertainment in the local hall. There, during the show, more bottles were sold.

When Houdini and Bess joined the show, business was bad. Doc Hill told them that he was encountering stubborn sales resistance from the people of Kansas. The trouble was that they were too healthy; none of them ever seemed to ail anything, or if they did they were doing nothing about it. He liked the Houdinis' act; it quickly became the most popular part of the show, but it did not improve the sales of his medicines.

Then, in Galena, he had an idea. A professional medium was touring the district, drawing large audiences. Houdini had told him that all mediums were fakes and that he himself could match any of them. So Doc Hill suggested to Houdini that he did a seance as a special Sunday show at the Opera House. He offered top billing and Houdini agreed. He was billed as 'Houdini the Great'. The seance took place on 9 January, 1898. The Opera House was crowded. The lights were lowered and the seance began. A table floated through the air, untouched accordions played sweet music, and spirit faces appeared. All in all, the performance was a great success.

Doc Hill was delighted and the seance was incorporated into the show. Houdini tied in with it his Second Sight routine. Bess, as the medium, would go into a trance and he would control her most impressively. The messages that came from beyond the grave for members of the audience were startling in their accuracy. The audience did not know that Doc Hill had spent the day talking to the sexton, copying names and dates from gravestones, and listening to the gossip of the town as he had his beard trimmed in the barber's shop. But unfortunately for him the intense interest taken by the people of Kansas in the world beyond the grave seemed to be undermining even more their wish to take the necessary steps that would ensure them living longer in this one. No matter how fervently he exhorted them they would not buy his medicines, with the result that by the end of the month the show folded.

Houdini and Bess were again without a job. He wrote immediately to the Welsh Brothers, hoping it would not be too late to join the circus for the summer season. They were offered a contract for a six month tour. But the tour would not begin until April, and in the meantime they had to live. The seances he had given had been so successful that he decided for the time being to set up in the spiritualist business on his own account, moving from town to town and operating from rooming houses and small halls.

The itinerant medium was a feature of small town America. In the midwest, where Houdini began operating, they were particularly well-organised. He soon discovered that the shadowy world of the dead had been well charted by the spook crooks. Some of them shared a directory, listing the names of those who attended seances, together with details of their dead relatives. Some indexed the birth, marriage, and death notices in the local newspapers; hunted through court records of property and mortgages; and even posed as house to house salesmen in order to get a look at the family Bible, in which names and dates of births and deaths were recorded.

Houdini was too honest to be a spook crook. He tried to convince himself, as some of his fellow magicians had succeeded in doing, that since many people believed stage routines of telepathy and clairvoyance to be supernatural despite the disclaimers of the magicians who performed them, then why not let them go on believing? If something in the nature of mankind was satisfied by this yearning to believe, then why not profit by it? But right from the start his conscience troubled him. Before a seance began, he would look at the strained white faces of his clients, some dressed in mourning, all wanting messages, and he was filled with pity for them. Then he would put Bess into a trance, and the table would float, and the accordion play, and the spirit faces would glow benignly as the messages came through. He was astonished that people could be so easily fooled, indeed wanted to be fooled, so long as they could go away with a message from someone they loved. At times he himself played the part of the medium, and then the spirits wrote messages on slates even when both his hands were tied behind his back. For the most part these messages were vague, full of comfort and cheerfulness, but now and then he was compelled to give a message that was precise and meaningful. To his rational mind, such messages were no more than inspired guesses, amazing coincidences, but all the same they disturbed him.

He was ashamed of the deceitful way he was earning his living. He could not reconcile it with his own reverence for the dead. His clients were pitiful, trusting, some mentally disturbed, others half-crazed with grief. True, he was giving them comfort, but it was false comfort. All he was really doing was taking advantage of their sorrow. Let Joe Rinn pursue his quest for a genuine medium, if such a one existed. All he knew was that spiritualism as practised by the spook crooks could be loathsome, dangerous, and evil.

*

He was glad when April came and he could join the Welsh

Brothers' Circus. He introduced the Strait-Jacket Escape into his act, but had to abandon it because audiences were simply not interested. He still persisted with the Handcuff Escape, and his collection of metal restraints was growing all the time. He collected not only handcuffs but also leg-irons and any other manacles he could find. And he was constantly filing and altering his picks; refining them so that one could open several types of lock. This cut down on the number he had to hide. But again these escapes did not get across to the audience.

When the season ended in October he was really discouraged. He was twenty-four years old. He had been a professional magician for seven years and had touched the big-time only once, when he played a week at Tony Pastor's theatre. Back in New York he talked of other work. Bess's brother-in-law offered to get him a job with the manufacturer of Yale locks. The prospect appealed to him. The job would give him a settled life with his mother, and moreover he was fascinated by locks. He could see himself absorbed at the locksmith's bench, mastering every lock. He was convinced that a pick could be made for any lock however intricate. Perhaps he would be allowed to design his own locks, so complex that they would baffle all experts, yet yield to the pressure of a simple pick.

Tempted as he was, his ambition to be the greatest magician in the world was too strong. He knew he had the makings of a good mystifying act, and that one day the breakthrough must surely come. A letter from Kohl & Middleton's, the dime museum in Chicago, decided his immediate future. They asked him to fill in for a few weeks. He liked Chicago; he had always been lucky there, so he left New York at once. In Chicago he could think of nothing but the Handcuff Escape. He was convinced that if in some way he could dramatise this he would capture the interest of audiences. So he revived the idea of a tie-in with the police that he had practised with varying success during his tour with 'The American Gaiety Girls'. He got the management to introduce him to some newspaper reporters. He told the reporters that he could release himself from any regulation police restraint. They took him to the police station, where he challenged the police to try to hold him. He escaped from all their handcuffs, and on 5 January, 1899, the incident was reported in the *Journal*.

The publicity paid off; it was the 'Challenge' that did it. Now from the stage of Kohl & Middleton's he challenged anyone in the audience to bind him with handcuffs or leg-irons; to submit him to their own restraints and he would escape from them. The audience were intrigued. It struck them that restraints supplied by bona fide, ticket-buying members of the public could not be doctored. But for Houdini there was a snag. Handcuffs and leg-irons were not part of the everyday impedimenta of ordinary private citizens; these were not the sort of articles they happened to have about them. So Houdini had to plant a few with confederates in the audience. But the rest of the audience were not to know this and the 'Challenge' made them sit up and take notice. In the 'Challenge' Houdini found the gimmick he had been seeking.

Bess and he were on the road again, the road of dime museums, but this time he was sure he was going somewhere. At St Paul, Minnesota, the act was noticed by Martin Beck, booker for the Orpheum vaudeville circuit. He liked Metamorphosis and the Challenge Handcuff Escape. He suspected, however, that the cuffs were doctored and so he bought a few pairs and sent them onstage. These were snapped on Houdini's wrists and arms. He released himself and emerged from the cabinet with the cuffs still locked. Beck was impressed.

He offered Houdini a tour at sixty dollars a week, but told him that he must re-structure his act. Beck thought it was too cluttered. In addition to Metamorphosis and the Challenge Handcuff Escape, Houdini did magic tricks—reaching into the flame of a candle and producing a red silk handkerchief; breaking a borrowed watch and restoring it; swallowing his needles and bringing them out threaded. In Beck's judgement, Houdini was trying to pack too much into his fifteen minutes. He told him to cut out the magic, with the possible exception of the Needle Trick. It distracted the audience and prevented him from building up a dramatic effect. He wanted no more than two thrillers in the act—Metamorphosis and the Challenge Handcuff Escape.

To Houdini this was surprising advice and not altogether welcome. He had never thought of his career solely in terms of escapology. His master was Robert-Houdin, purest of magicians, his aim was to have a full two-hour magic show. Now he was in danger of ending up as a sideshow on some carnival midway. But he had to go along with Beck, as he was hardly in a position to refuse a tour with the Orpheum circuit, the most important circuit in the west, with its chain of first class vaudeville theatres stretching from Chicago to San Francisco.

Beck certainly did not see the makings of an elegant suave magician in this man who mumbled ungrammatically. And while he was impressed by Houdini's talent, he had reservations about his showmanship. Houdini struck him as a shy withdrawn person, somewhat out of place in the world of show business. He expressed these doubts to Houdini, telling him that the art of showmanship was getting people to talk about you to such an extent that everyone wanted to see your act. This meant bragging about yourself, blowing your own trumpet, banging your own drum. Houdini listened intently. Beck was to find that he had misjudged his man. True, Houdini was quiet and reflective, inhibited by his lack of formal education, but he was also egotistical and ambitious to an inordinate degree. Beck was to find, as the world was to find, that no one could brag about himself, or blow his own trumpet, or bang his own drum louder and longer than Houdini.

He started by claiming from the stages of the Orpheum theatres that the Challenge Handcuff Escape was his own invention and his alone, which indeed it was. He denounced all other handcuff acts as imitations, which indeed they were not. He tried to set up police station escapes in every town he played, and after each escape he asked the police chief to sign a document certifying what he had done. He told his audiences that all other handcuff performers used doctored cuffs and duplicate keys and then restricted their escapes to their own handcuffs. Only he, Houdini, was willing to escape from any type of restraint submitted by any member of the audience.

Taking on all comers had its risks. In different states he had to be on guard in case a make of handcuff was brought onstage of which he had no knowledge. This risk was minimised by his stipulation that all cuffs had to be of regulation pattern. He had now mastered most of these, for his study of restraints never ceased. Nor did the refining of his picks. He was not only increasing the multiplicity of their use but also making them smaller and smaller so that they could be more easily hidden.

The re-structured act was a great success. Bess was still a part of it, but as an assistant not an equal. They were no longer billed as 'The Houdinis'; only his name appeared on the posters and he styled himself 'Houdini: The King of Handcuffs'. By the time he reached California in the summer, his salary had been raised to ninety dollars a week.

Newspaper publicity was what he sought and newspaper publicity was what he got, although it was not always favourable. While playing in San Francisco, he escaped from various restraints at the police station. After he had left the city, the *Examiner* published a feature which claimed to expose the secrets of his handcuff escapes, stating that there was nothing marvellous about them, that only an extra key or a pick was needed and that, in any event, he had only escaped from a selected range of restraints at the police station. This attack did not disturb Houdini. He already agreed with Barnum's dictum that any publicity was better than no publicity, and in any case it is highly probable that he had orchestrated the attack himself.

When he played a return date at San Francisco, he challenged the police to bind him in every restraint they possessed. On 13 July, 1899 he went to the police station, where, to the surprise and amusement of the hard-boiled officers and reporters, he began to strip off his clothes. When he was completely naked, he asked them where were the duplicate keys or picks? Everyone had stopped smiling now, for naked as he was he had about him an air of superhuman qualities, the boldness of a man who would attempt great things. He challenged the doctor to find anything on him. The doctor ran his hands over every part of him from the top of his head to his toes, his fingers exploring every orifice. He found nothing secreted on the naked body.

Where then had Houdini hidden his picks? He could have

concealed them by misdirection or sleight of hand. The examination had started with his head and finished with his feet. After his hands had been examined, he could have distracted the attention of the doctor in order to touch a certain part of his body with a quick movement. This gesture could be a trick to recover some tiny pick stuck there with a piece of wax. He would then be holding a pick in a hand already searched. Some of his picks were no more than a short length of thin wire; these could have been hidden in his crinkly hair. Most officials wore black, especially doctors. He could have made a tiny black cloth bag to contain the picks and equip it with a hook. He was skilful enough to hook this unnoticed on the doctor's back and retrieve it after the examination. He could have used any of these methods, or a combination of them, or even a method unknown to anyone. After all, the problem of hiding the picks could not have been too difficult for a man who could hide fifty needles inside his mouth.

After the doctor's examination Houdini's hands were shackled behind his back, his ankles were manacled and between these ten pairs of handcuffs were linked. He was carried to a closet which had previously been searched, dumped on the floor and left there. Ten minutes later he appeared, free of all the restraints, which were still locked one within the other. The reporters left to tell their readers what they had witnessed. As the people of San Francisco read the story, their imagination was gripped and strange long-buried, elemental feelings stirred within them, for a deed that belonged to the age of mythological heroes had occurred in a bustling, industrial city in the closing days of the nineteenth century. A man, naked against the world, bound in chains, deprived of all help, had yet restored himself to freedom.

Chapter Three

NO ORDINARY MAN

In the twentieth century Houdini was to perform even greater deeds. When the century began he was earning one hundred and twenty-five dollars a week. The Orpheum tour had ended in the autumn of 1899 and now he was touring the Keith circuit, the leading vaudeville chain in the east. Among other cities, he played Boston and New York. But when the tour ended in February neither the Orpheum nor the Keith circuit was anxious to re-book him. In their opinion, his act had been exploited for all it was worth. He was determined never to go back to the dime museums and beer halls, so he resolved to do what other American entertainers had done before him—gain a European reputation and then return. The approval of London, Paris, and Berlin was valued in America, which even in this opening year of the twentieth century was a naive country, with an enormous inferiority complex where Europe was concerned. He was in agony over leaving his mother, not knowing when he would see her again, but he was compelled to go. He intended to sail with Bess for England, for London, centre of the entertainment world and gateway to Europe. His name was unknown there and he had not a single engagement ahead of him, but he did have a sheaf of police certificates, a book of press cuttings, and an all-consuming desire for recognition.

On 30 May, 1900, he sailed from New York, and the ship had no sooner left the pier than he was stricken with seasickness. By the third day he was delirious, threatening to throw himself overboard. Bess was so concerned that she took the precaution of tying him to his berth. Seasickness was to prove one of the great trials of his life; it became so chronic that even the act of buying a boat ticket could bring on an attack of nausea.

In London he called on agents and theatre managers, showing them his press cuttings and police certificates. No one showed much enthusiasm, until he met Harry Day, a young agent who had recently set up in business. Day thought the act had possibilities and tried to sell it to C. Dundas Slater, manager of the Alhambra, one of the best variety theatres in London. Slater gave Houdini an audition, but was not happy about him. He believed the trouble lay in the remoteness of Houdini's claims. Certificates from police chiefs in San Francisco and Chicago carried little weight in Britain, where America was regarded as so corrupt that collusion between Houdini and the police would be taken for granted.

But Houdini, as always, was prepared. Before leaving America he had mastered British handcuffs; there were only eight models and he had found none of them very difficult. He suggested that Slater arrange for him to escape from handcuffs in some London police station. Slater chose the most prestigious of them all, Scotland Yard, headquarters of the Criminal Investigation Department. Superintendent Melville, a friend of his, arranged the test. Houdini went to Scotland Yard, where Melville handcuffed him round a metal pillar, saying that he would be back in a couple of hours to release him. But Houdini was free before Melville reached the door.

The Scotland Yard escape gave Houdini the publicity he needed. Within three weeks of arriving unknown in England, he opened at the Alhambra billed as 'The Handcuff King'. The opening night saw some extraordinary incidents. He had no sooner begun his act than a man in the stalls jumped to his feet and denounced him as a fraud. Houdini advised the man to be quiet. But the man would not be quiet; he strode down the aisle and mounted the stage. There he introduced himself to the puzzled audience as the Great Cirnoc. He told them that he was the original Handcuff King and, pointing to Houdini, he again denounced him as a fraud and, moreover, not only a fraud but an impostor, since Houdini was not an American and indeed had never even set foot in America.

While the murmuring audience were digesting this startling

information, another man stood up in the stalls. He was tall and distinguished. He introduced himself as Mr Chauncey M. Depew, lawyer, politician, and citizen of good standing in the republic of the United States. He wished to state categorically that he had seen Houdini perform in America, that he was not a fraud, and that he most certainly was a citizen of that great country. At which he resumed his seat.

Houdini now spoke up. Holding aloft a pair of handcuffs, he said that there was one way to prove who was telling the truth. He told the audience that the handcuffs were known as the Bean Giant, the most secure of all American restraints; the invention of Captain Bean, of Boston, who claimed that it was impossible to open them without the proper key. There was a standing prize of five thousand dollars for the person who could unlock them by any other means. He, Houdini, had unlocked them, but could not claim the reward because he would not reveal his method. Turning to the Great Cirnoc he challenged him to escape from the Bean Giant and claim the five thousand dollars.

Cirnoc hesitated. Then he said that he would be happy to escape from the Bean Giant, but only after Houdini had demonstrated that he could do so. Houdini agreed and Cirnoc fastened the cuffs on him. Houdini entered his cabinet and in a few seconds emerged free. Cirnoc could refuse no longer. He held out his hands and Houdini secured him. But try as he might Cirnoc could not unfasten the cuffs and eventually Houdini had to release him. Cirnoc took his defeat in good part, shaking Houdini warmly by the hand, a gesture intended to appeal to the best sporting instincts of the British. The audience responded with prolonged appreciative applause, but there were some among them who had the uneasy suspicion that they had been bamboozled by a Yankee trick.

Houdini's act was widely talked about and Slater retained him indefinitely at the Alhambra. Week after week Houdini kept the interest alive by varying his repertoire of escapes. He claimed to accept all challenges, but he left nothing to chance and escaped only from restraints that he had previously tested. This meant spending his days in locksmiths and scrap metal yards, searching out manacles and other restraints. From early July until the end of August he played to packed houses. He could have stayed longer, but Day had made some bookings in Germany.

Dresden was the first city he visited in Germany. At the police headquarters he escaped from every type of handcuff put on him. The chief of police gave him the official certificate he demanded, but the authorities were disturbed and the reporting of the incident was reticent. On his opening night at the Central Theatre, he escaped from the formidable leg irons and manacles of the Mathildegasse prison, the locks of which alone weighed forty pounds. The audience was the most enthusiastic he had ever had, and the fact that he addressed them in German endeared him to them even more. Dresden could not have enough of him. He was booked to appear next at the Wintergarten in Berlin. The manager of the Central Theatre appealed to the Wintergarten to be allowed to retain him for a further month, but this was refused for the people of Berlin were eager to see him.

He arrived in Berlin in October and escaped naked from all restraints at the police headquarters. The official verification was signed by Count von Windheim, the highest ranking police officer in Germany. During his month's engagement, the Wintergarten was beseiged by crowds. Berlin, like Dresden, did not want to let him go. Now the Wintergarten appealed to Roanacher's in Vienna for Houdini to be retained through November. Roanacher's agreed reluctantly, but demanded an indemnity of four thousand marks, a sum equal to Houdini's salary for a month.

In Berlin Houdini accepted all challenges, but he had to be careful that he never accepted one he could not meet. His act depended on total success. One failure, only one, could ruin him. But he always prepared carefully. During the Berlin engagement, he spent all his spare time at Mueller's, the locksmith on the Mittelstrasse. There he worked for up to ten hours a day, studying locks. Mueller ordered locks for him from all parts of Germany, locks of every type and period. There was much to learn as Germany had a longer history of restraint than America. He studied not only restraints but every conceivable kind of lock— ancient ones to treasure chests, torture chambers, and city gates; modern ones to the most complex safes and strong rooms. He could soon pick hundreds of three and four lever locks as quickly as they could be opened with a key, and he only needed four tiny picks two centimetres long. Some three or four lever locks were of a peculiar pattern in which a post in the keyhole prevented strong wire from entering. For these he devised several different shaped picks from piano wire. Then he went on to open locks that contained five or six levers. He mastered every lock that Mueller brought to him: whatever men had most cunningly devised to protect themselves and their property, and to restrain those they feared; he learned to open them all. He became so skilful that some locks seemed to open at his touch.

In December he was back in London, topping the bill again at the Alhambra. In the previous month London had welcomed another young American magician when Howard Thurston opened at the Palace Theatre. In his own country Thurston was already being spoken of as a serious rival to Kellar, and since the death of Herrmann the Great, Kellar had been acknowledged as the finest magician in America. Some months before his death, Herrmann the Great had nominated his nephew, Leon, as his successor. Leon had gone into partnership with Herrmann's widow, Adelaide. He cultivated the family trademark of satanic black moustache and beard; he also styled himself Herrmann the Great. But he was never to achieve the stature of his uncle, and Kellar had no serious competition until the advent of Thurston. During his London engagement, Thurston amazed audiences by his dexterity with cards, particularly his 'Rising Card' trick, where the cards soared upwards from his hands, controlled by invisible threads, but seemingly moving freely in space. The Prince of Wales had gone backstage to congratulate him.

Houdini was sensitive to the fact that despite all his success he had no standing in the world of pure magic. No royalty or aristocracy attended his performances. Perhaps escapes from manacles had no interest for people whose lives had never been restrained. Certainly the bulk of his audience was working class. Marxists were soon to see in him the living symbol of the common man freeing himself from economic bondage. Such symbolism was unconscious on Houdini's part; he did not see his art in terms of the class struggle. For unknown reasons he had taken an unknown road, which was leading him away from the world of elegant magicians and their royal patrons, a world he admired and envied. But he was compelled to dedicate himself to a life of discipline, pain, and endurance; to the task of seeking out all restraints that he might break through them, dimly apprehending that some day, somewhere, when the last restraint had been conquered, he would find himself in a world to which he truly belonged.

*

As the first year of the twentieth century ended, offers poured in for Houdini from impresarios all over Europe. There was work enough to keep him occupied for years, and it seemed to him that he would never see his mother again. While he yearned for her, the whole of Britain was concerned about another little old lady. Queen Victoria was on her deathbed, and when she died on 22 January, 1901, she left a great void in the hearts of her people. She had reigned for sixty-four years; it was difficult to imagine Britain without her. Houdini was in the tune with the prevailing mood of sorrow.

He understood it; a mother had died. He was moved by the signs of mourning in the street, the black draped shop windows, the flags at half-mast. So he would expect the whole world to mourn his mother.

One shop, as a mark of respect, displayed a gown designed for the Queen but never worn by her. When Houdini saw it, he was struck by the fact that the Queen must have been exactly the same shape and height as his mother. This pleased him. He went into the shop and offered to buy the gown. At first the manager was shocked, but Houdini's attitude was so respectful and the price he offered was so high that the manager agreed to sell the gown on the condition that it would never be worn in Britain.

In February Houdini toured the English provinces then left again for Germany. He played at Leipzig and Düsseldorf. Neither city wanted him to leave, but he had to move on as every city in

Germany wanted to see him. German magicians were quick to take advantage of the craze, and challenge handcuff acts sprang up all over the country. This infuriated Houdini, for his imitators used doctored cuffs and so debased his act. He exposed them whenever he could, but there were too many of them and he could not play in every town. So he decided that if anyone was going to cash in on his success that person would be his own brother. Dash was performing as a magician under the name of Hardeen. Houdini sent him a telegram, advising him to come to Europe. Dash arrived when Houdini was playing in Hamburg. They arranged that Dash would play the towns Houdini could not visit, using Metamorphosis and the handcuff releases. They would play in competition with each other, while keeping their relationship a secret.

When Dash came to Germany, he brought their mother with him and now Houdini was content. Hour after hour he sat with her, telling her of his triumphs. Sometimes he rested his head on her lap while she stroked his hair; sometimes he pressed his ear to her heart to listen again to its reassuring beat. He took her to her native Hungary, to Budapest, and there, in the leading hotel, among the fountains and ornate rococo furnishing of the palm court, his mother, dressed in a gown made for a queen, received her relatives and old friends. For Houdini this was a day of deep contentment and happiness.

But the time quickly came for him to resume his German tour, so he kissed his mother goodbye over and over again, and reluctantly put her on a boat for America. In May he visited the ugly, sprawling industrial city of Essen, where skilled men of the Krupps steel foundry forged special manacles and challenged him to escape from them. He accepted the challenge. On the night it seemed as though the entire work force of the vast foundry had turned up to see him. They overwhelmed the theatre, and those unable to get in rioted outside. Peace was restored only when Houdini promised to repeat the escape the following night. He escaped from the manacles within a few minutes.

On the final night the packed theatre shouted for Houdini and Houdini alone; they did not want the other acts on the bill. The challenge he accepted that night was a hard one. The most skilled workers in metal had again brought all their ingenuity to the forging of restraints to secure him. His arms and legs were manacled and a metal collar padlocked round his neck. From this collar hung chains, which were tightened to force him into a squatting position. He had to be carried into his cabinet and left there. He escaped in eleven minutes. The audience went wild with delight, and he was crowned with a laurel wreath.

At the police headquarters in Dortmund he escaped from the heavy irons worn by the murderer, Glowisky, when beheaded three days previously. At Hanover, Count von Schwerin, the chief of police, was disturbed by Houdini's reputation, and wanted to defeat him. So he challenged him to escape from a special strait-jacket used for violent prisoners. It was made of heavy canvas reinforced with thick leather, far more difficult than any he had previously encountered. But he allowed himself to be bound in it. The escape proved to be the hardest he had yet experienced. Every movement was torture. Von Schwerin was quietly jubilant; he believed that at last this strange man had been mastered. Houdini struggled in pain for one and a half hours before releasing himself. He had won, but the agony of that struggle was to haunt him for the rest of his life.

Count von Schwerin was not the only police officer to be disturbed by Houdini's triumphant progress through Germany. In Cologne, Werner Graff, after witnessing Houdini's escapes from all the restraints at the police headquarters, felt compelled to put a stop to him. So he wrote an article which appeared in the *Rheinische Zeitung*, of 25 July, in which he denounced Houdini as a charlatan. Graff stated that Houdini by trickery and faking had escaped from some easy restraints, yet he claimed in his publicity that he could escape from police restraints of any kind. Such a claim was false and Houdini should be prosecuted for fraud.

The motive for this attack was not malice on Graff's part, but his fear, shared by von Schwerin and other police officers, that Houdini was undermining their authority and encouraging hopes of escape in the minds of prisoners. Houdini, for his part, could not ignore the attack; the article had been widely reprinted throughout Germany. His act depended on the co-operation of the police. If they were to denounce him as a fraud in every town he visited, his future would be in jeopardy. Yet to seek legal redress against the police in so authoritarian a country as Germany was not a course of action that held much prospect of success. But he believed he had no other choice, and so he engaged a German lawyer, Dr Schreiber, and sued Werner Graff and the Cologne police for criminal libel.

Harry Day had arranged a season in Paris, and in December, 1901, Houdini opened there at the Olympic Theatre. He was to receive the highest salary ever paid to a foreign performer. In Paris his publicity took a bizarre form. He hired seven men to sit in line outside a café on one of the busiest boulevards. At regular intervals they removed their hats and bowed their heads to the passing crowds. They were all bald headed and on each pate was a letter which altogether spelled 'HOUDINI'

Now that he was in France he could at last pay homage to his hero, Robert-Houdin. He wrote to the surviving relative, the widow of Robert-Houdin's son, asking for permission to place a wreath on the tomb of her illustrious father-in-law. The letter was not answered. He was furious at the snub, but he did not let it prevent him from travelling to Blois, where Robert-Houdin was buried. There he placed his wreath on the tomb and stood in silent meditation, while the photographer he had brought with him from Paris recorded the scene. But the occasion had been spoiled for him by the snub. He could not forget it; it was to rankle for years.

January 1902 found him in Amsterdam, where naked and bowed down with heavy chains he was locked in a prison cell. To the amazement of all the officials, he broke out of the irons and the cell in fifteen minutes. Escaping naked not only from manacles but also from a locked cell was a logical development of his art. Even before leaving America, when escaping from handcuffs at police stations, he had surreptitiously examined the locks on the prison cells, working out methods of escaping. The main problem was the hiding of a pick too large to conceal on his body. In Kansas City he had escaped naked from a cell, but he had not made this a regular stunt in other towns as he had not yet perfected his techniques. These usually involved an inspection of the cell before attempting an escape. Then under the pretext of examining the door, he could plant a pick under the lock casing, securing it with wax; or he could drop the pick into a crack in the floor, or outside the cell door close to the bars. Throughout his European tour he had been experimenting with these techniques, and in Amsterdam had felt confident enough to escape from a locked cell.

This new development disturbed the police even more. It was already known to them in Germany, when in February he returned to Cologne, where his libel case against Werner Graff and the Cologne police was due to be heard. Graff told the court that Houdini had claimed he could open police restraints of any kind and he had not proved this claim, therefore he was a fraud. Houdini stated that as he had never failed to open any restraint the police had used against him his claim could be fairly made, therefore he was not a fraud, Graff declared that he would prove Houdini a fraud by binding him with a chain fastened with a police regulation lock. Graff had searched out the hardest restraint he could find, one he knew Houdini had never attempted publicly. Houdini examined the restraint and agreed to be bound. The lock was one he had mastered at the locksmith's bench. Again his careful preparation gave him the advantage. But he did not want his technique to be revealed in front of the crowded court, so he asked the judge for permission to escape in private. His request was denied. He attempted to lessen the odds by pleading that he should release himself only before the judge, jury and counsel. This request was allowed, and while the court was being cleared and everyone's attention distracted, Houdini escaped so quickly that no one had any idea how he had done it.

He won his case, but the matter was by no means finished. Graff appealed to a higher court, and in July his appeal was heard. He had had a pair of manacles constructed by master mechanic Kroch, the finest locksmith in Germany. The lock was so constructed that once closed it could not be opened even with its own key. Graff challenged Houdini to escape from the manacles and Houdini accepted the challenge. It was a worrying situation for him. He never cared to accept a challenge unless he had previous knowledge of the lock concerned. If he were to fail, his reputation was finished. This time the judge allowed him to retire to a private room. In less than four minutes he returned to the court and handed the opened manacles to the judge.

The final verdict was handed down on 24 October. Werner Graff was found guilty of insulting Houdini. He was fined thirty marks and ordered to pay all legal costs. But Houdini was not content with this. Having won, he was determined to exploit the result for all it was worth. He demanded and obtained a public apology to be published in all the newspapers, and he incorporated the apology into a dramatic publicity poster, which depicted him standing manacled before a judge, learned counsel, and assembled police officers.

And what were the police to think of him now? He presented a problem for which they had no solution. They accounted themselves lucky that he was an honest man, otherwise he could have been the master criminal of all time. He could enter or leave any building. He could open any safe. And even if captured no prison could hold him. He would have to be mutilated, his hands and feet cut off, but even that might not stop him. Society would have to kill him, for his powers were beyond its control.

*

In April 1903 he returned for a brief visit to America, to celebrate his twenty-eighth birthday with his mother and to discuss his future with Martin Beck. He arrived pale and shaken, having been seasick during the entire voyage. Beck was so busy that Houdini could only talk to him on trains. They travelled from Washington to Pittsburgh and back, talking, in a Pullman car. Houdini wanted to know whether he should cash in on his European success and play a season in the States. Beck advised against this. Europe still wanted him so much and this could only increase American interest in him. So Houdini returned to Europe and was seasick all the way. In his agony, he believed that he would never walk on land again.

He had so many bookings in Europe that he reckoned he could stay there for at least another three years. There was no danger of him living on a reputation already earned, for his ambition compelled him to extend his repertoire of escapes both inside the theatre and out. Wherever he went, he performed some outside stunt, brilliant and imaginative, intended to bring in the crowds to his theatre performances. In Holland he had himself tied to the wing of a windmill, attempting to escape as it rotated. In England he broke out of the jail at Leicester built by Oliver Cromwell. At Sheffield he escaped from the cell that had held Charles Peace, himself a notorious jail-breaker.

And from the stage of every theatre he continued to accept challenges to be bound with chains and ropes. As always, the trouble was that one failure could ruin him. So far his skill and knowledge had enabled him to meet all challenges, but there was always a risk. In Halifax a local magician bound him with ropes. For the first time Houdini experienced a dangerous tie, and he had to struggle desperately to escape. In Blackburn he was savagely tied by a sadistic instructor in physical education.

But most of the challenges were concerned with handcuffs, and this was a field he had completely mastered. This was why he was so infuriated that all over Europe 'Handcuff Kings' were boasting that they had taken the title from him. Whenever possible, he exposed them. While in Holland he had travelled all the way to Dortmund, where an escape artist named Kleppini was claiming that he had won a handcuff duel with him. Houdini went to Kleppini's performance disguised with a moustache. As Kleppini boasted of his triumph, Houdini stood up and shouted, 'Not true, not true.' 'How do you know?' Kleppini asked. Houdini ripped off his moustache in a dramatic gesture and exclaimed, 'I am Houdini!' The delighted audience cheered him. In the contest that followed they saw that Kleppini was no match for him. Such encounters delighted Houdini, but to expose all imitators would be a full-time job. So he issued a 'CHALLENGE

TO THE WORLD', offering a prize of one thousand pounds to anyone who could duplicate his releases under test conditions. The challenge was never taken up.

In the spring of 1903 he was back in Germany. At Cologne he was given a great reception as the man who had triumphed over the police, and it was at Cologne that Franz Kukol joined him as his assistant. Houdini needed someone who could liaise with the police and also help him with his backstage arrangements. Kukol was the perfect choice, a man of military manners and methods. He had been an officer in the Austrian army and could speak several languages. His background was somewhat mysterious, but it was believed that at one time he had worked in a circus. With his military bearing and black waxed upturned moustache he was an impressive figure. He handled people with authority and browbeat underlings. He was a pianist and arranged the music for Houdini's act, rehearsing the orchestra for the cues. His duties made it necessary for him to know some details of Houdini's escape methods, so he had to sign a document swearing that he would never reveal any secrets.

While in Cologne Houdini met Alexander Heimburger, the magician. They had many long conversations together. It was Heimburger who first told him that Robert-Houdin had not been so original as he had made himself out to be; that he had taken the tricks of past magicians and claimed that he had invented them. Houdini listened astounded to Heimburger's revelations. Heimburger told him of magicians from whom Robert-Houdin had stolen their reputations. He told him of the great Bamberg family, who for generation after generation had been Court Magicians to the Kings of Holland, performing many of the tricks Robert-Houdin had claimed as his own. He told him of Pinetti, who had perfected the Second Sight routine in the eighteenth century, decades before Robert-Houdin. He told him of Philippe, who had linked and unlinked glittering silver rings, seemingly passing solid metal through solid metal; of Doebler, who had fired a pistol, and hundreds of candles in the theatre had instantaneously burst into flame; of John Henry Anderson, 'The Great Wizard of the North', who had been the first to have a bullet fired pointblank at him and catch it in his teeth, and who had altered the course of magic ten years before Robert-Houdin. And he also told him of the legendary wizard, Wiljalba Frikell, who had been the first to discard the oriental gown considered essential to the stage magician and had appeared in conventional evening dress, and who had given the first pure sleight-of-hand performance without cumbersome draperies and apparatus. Robert-Houdin had claimed both these innovations as his own.

When Houdini heard all this, he was dismayed. He felt contaminated by having taken the name of a man so contemptuous of tradition; an apostate who had denied his debt to the long line of wonder-workers dating back to the ancient wizards who had performed in the courts of the Pharaohs. He vowed that he would became the custodian of that tradition. He would build up the finest library of magic in the world. He would become a scholar. He would write books. And when he had gathered sufficient evidence, he would unmask that villain, Robert-Houdin. It may be that Robert-Houdin deserved to be unmasked, and it may be that Houdini's motive was partly vindictive, remembering the snub he had received from the widow of the magician's son.

But Heimburger had also given him happy news, news that had made him jump up from his chair in joy and disbelief. Heimburger told him that Wiljalba Frikell, one of the greatest of all magicians, was still alive, an old, old man living near Dresden. When Houdini heard this, the greatest desire of his life was to visit Frikell. He wrote to him, begging for an interview, but received no reply. He wrote letter after letter, but still no reply. Undeterred, he decided to go in person to Frikell's house.

At Dresden he was told that the old magician was now a recluse and would see no one. Houdini went to the house and knocked on the door, but the door remained unopened. He knocked again more insistently, for he was certain that Frikell was inside, but still no one responded. He hammered on the door again and again. Frikell's wife appeared at an upstairs window. Houdini begged her to allow him to see Frikell, but she shook her head. He told her that he had a question he must ask. So passionate was his pleading that the tears flowed down her cheeks, but she continued to shake her head. Behind her, out of sight, the old magician sat listening impassively. Houdini went away, disappointed.

In May he went to Russia and played both in Moscow and St Petersburg. In the streets of Moscow he saw carettes, horse-drawn vans, heavily locked and bolted, carrying prisoners for transportation to Siberia. He went to the chief of the Moscow police and asked permission to escape from one. Permission was granted, and he escaped stark naked. When the police inspected the van, it was still locked. They were determined that no word of this would get about, so the chief of police would neither give him a certificate nor allow the escape to be publicised in any way. It seemed to Houdini that Russia itself was one vast prison and he was glad to leave the country.

From Russia he had continued to bombard Frikell with letters, and eventually his persistence was rewarded. Frikell's wife wrote to tell him that the old magician would see him. Houdini was overjoyed, for there remained the unanswered question, the one he had hoped to put to Herrmann the Great. Could the relentless application of technique bring into play some psychic force which caused an effect that was truly magic? He knew that when he performed Metamorphosis he moved so quickly that it seemed he had left his own body. And sometimes, when faced with a difficult lock, he had breathed a prayer and then mastered the lock. He was reluctant to attribute this to psychic help, for he had known all along that that particular pick was the one to open that lock. Still the question had to be asked.

On Saturday, 8 October, Houdini called at Frikell's house and the magician's wife opened the door. She asked him to enter, telling him that he was being waited for. She showed him into a room, where Frikell sat in a chair, dressed in his best clothes, surrounded by his medals and decorations. Houdini was indeed being waited for, but another caller, Death, had arrived one hour before him.

*

In November Houdini was in England. At Huddersfield, Sheffield, and Liverpool he escaped naked from prison cells. In London, in the arena of the vast Hippodrome circus, he escaped from the manacles worn by Count de Lorge, who had been imprisoned in the Bastille for fifteen years; and from two pairs of handcuffs that had held Jack Sheppard, the highwayman. And the wonderful thing was that all the locks were still locked after his escape. They did not appear to have been damaged or interfered with in any way.

His Challenge act was now the greatest draw in Europe, yet strangely enough the audience never actually saw him do anything. He disappeared into his cabinet and remained hidden there for sometimes more than an hour. They never saw him release himself. They spent the time looking at the cabinet and listening to the orchestra. Yet they sat enthralled, for they were convinced that he was about to do something remarkable and they identified themselves with him. None of them wanted him to fail. They worried about him when he was out of sight, longing and praying for him to succeed. Sometimes he would stay hidden after he had released himself, waiting until what he judged was the right moment before revealing himself. When he emerged and they roared their delight, they were acclaiming not only him but also themselves, for what they had witnessed was not so much a variety turn as a celebration of the human spirit triumphing over every obstacle.

But there were growing rumours of a challenge which if Houdini were to accept he would surely fail. A master locksmith in Birmingham had spent five years of his life devising a lock which he claimed no mortal man could pick. He had incorporated this into a pair of handcuffs. The *Daily Illustrated Mirror* had purchased the handcuffs. These were examined by London's best locksmiths, who all agreed that never in their experience had they seen such wonderful mechanism. The *Mirror* challenged Houdini to escape from the cuffs and he accepted the challenge, although he admitted that he did not like the look of them.

c

The trial took place on 17 March, 1904, at the Hippodrome, before a packed house of four thousand spectators. When Houdini stepped into the arena, he was given a great ovation. A journalist from the *Mirror* snapped the handcuffs on his wrists and turned the key six times to secure the bolt as firmly as possible. Houdini retired to his cabinet and the orchestra began to play. Twenty minutes passed and still the orchestra played on. Then Houdini put his head out of the cabinet. This was the signal for an outburst of cheering, which turned to groans of disappointment when it was learned that he was only trying to get a better look at the lock. The orchestra broke into a dreamy waltz as Houdini once more disappeared into the cabinet.

At thirty-five minutes he again came out, this time to ask for a cushion as his knees were hurting. A cushion was handed to him and he pulled it through into the cabinet. For twenty minutes more the orchestra played on, then he emerged once more, still handcuffed. The audience groaned as this was noticed, and it also seemed to them that he was exhausted. He asked the journalist for the handcuffs to be removed so that he could take his coat off. The request was refused on the grounds that although Houdini had seen how the cuffs were locked he had not seen how they were unlocked, and this could perhaps give him some advantage. Then, to the delight of the audience, Houdini manoeuvred a penknife from his waistcoat pocket, opened it with his teeth, and turning his coat inside out over his head, proceeded to cut it to pieces. These he discarded and re-entered the cabinet.

It was announced that Houdini had been manacled for one hour. Far from being bored, everyone was trembling with suppressed excitement. Ten minutes more. The orchestra was just finishing a stirring march when, with a cry of victory, Houdini bounded from the cabinet, holding the handcuffs aloft—free!

A mighty roar went up from the crowd. Men waved their hats, shook hands, and even embraced one another. Women waved their handkerchiefs, sobbing with gladness and relief. A group of men shouldered Houdini and bore him in triumph round the arena, and he himself was sobbing, sobbing bitterly, as though his heart would break.

*

At the end of May, he returned to America to visit his mother. Theatres there wanted him, but as they were unwilling to pay the money he could command in Europe Martin Beck advised him to bide his time. During this visit he was initiated as a member of the Society of American Magicians. The ceremony took place in the famous back room of Martinka's Magic Shop on Sixth Avenue, where all the great magicians congregated.

He bought a large brownstone house, 278 West 113th Street, in the German section of Harlem; four storeys high with twenty-six rooms. His mother gently protested when he moved her there from her modest apartment. She wondered why he needed so large a house as Bess and he had no children. But he had begun collecting material on magic. The crates of books and pamphlets he had brought with him from Europe already filled three rooms. He needed space for his collection to grow, and it was also his intention that when his wanderings were over this house should be his home for the rest of his life.

And he prepared the place that was to house him after death. He bought a family burial plot at Machpelah Cemetery, Cypress Hills, Brooklyn, and moved there the bodies of his father, maternal grandmother, and brother Herman. He examined their remains before these were re-interred and noted that Herman's teeth were in splendid condition. He too would lie there eventually and also Bess and his mother. While he could contemplate his own death and that of Bess, he could not bear the thought of his mother dying, although he realised that in the nature of things she would most probably die first. So he prayed that he might be allowed to die before her.

At the end of August, after less than three months in America, he returned to Britain. He was so popular with British audiences that Harry Day had arranged for him to be paid not a straight salary but a percentage of the profits. This could bring him in as much as two thousand dollars a week. Basically his act had never altered during the four years he had been in Europe.

CHALLENGE

Houdini, Esq.,
     Hippodrome, Blackpool.

Dear Sir,—As our Chief Constable, Mr. J. C.
Derham was unable to hold you in the Police
Station Cells yesterday, and as you claim that
nothing can hold you, allow me to say that I
can make an ordinary

PACKING CASE

of one

INCH DEAL

and can

NAIL YOU UP!

as well as rope up the box so that you cannot
make your escape.

If you accept this challenge, I will send
along the box, for you to examine, but to prevent you preparing the box while in your
possession, I insist on the right of re-nailing
up each BOARD before you enter.

Awaiting your reply I remain,

THOMAS HARTLEY.

Boro' Saw Mills,
     Middle Street and Marshall Street, Blackpool.

HOUDINI
ACCEPTS ABOVE CHALLENGE

For WEDNESDAY NIGHT, JUNE 14th, 1905,
at the HIPPODROME, BLACKPOOL.

Everyone allowed to bring along Hammer and Nails to assist in nailing Houdini in!

TO-NIGHT, Wednesday
HIPPODROME, BLACKPOOL.

PRINTED AT THE "HERALD" OFFICE. BLACKPOOL.

A typical Challenge Handbill

It comprised the Needle Trick, Metamorphosis, which he did with Bess, and the Challenge. He was always looking for variations of the Challenge to keep his act fresh, and he was now escaping from wooden packing boxes. During this trip to Britain he perfected his method of publicising and presenting the Packing Box Challenge.

In September, in Glasgow, he escaped from a wooden packing box in which he had been nailed down. He then encouraged the joinery firm of J. and G. Findlay to cast aspersions on his box, to say that it was not genuine, that it had been specially prepared. He manoeuvred them into challenging him to escape from a packing case constructed by themselves. He accepted their challenge on condition that the box was constructed to his specifications of the overall dimensions and thickness of wood. Then the city was flooded with handbills stating the terms of the challenge and his acceptance of them. The escape was advertised for a performance some nights ahead so that the packing box could be exhibited in the foyer of the theatre, where all who wished could examine it.

And there it was examined secretly by Houdini and Franz Kukol, when they crept stealthily into the empty theatre by night. They pulled out the long nails holding one of the side panels, snapped them short and then replaced them.

On the night of the performance, eight joiners employed by J. and G. Findlay nailed Houdini down in the box and secured it with ropes. When the cabinet had been placed round the box, Houdini pushed out the side panel and wriggled through. He then pulled out the shortened nails and replaced them with long nails, which he had previously hidden in the hollow metal supports of his cabinet together with an instrument for hammering them back into the packing box. The noise of the hammering could not be heard over the sound of the orchestra, which had been instructed to play breezy, brassy tunes throughout the escape.

After fifteen minutes he emerged from the cabinet, perspiring, dishevelled, and minus both his shoes. The audience of working people gave him a standing ovation. When he kissed his hands towards all those shining, rapturous faces, the shouts of approval and admiration grew even louder. The streets outside were crowded and he was carried shoulder-high to the house where he was lodging. Meanwhile, the eight joiners were dismantling the box to see whether it had been tampered with in any way and they found it exactly as they had constructed it.

And throughout Europe the ordinary people read of all these deeds of Houdini and wondered what manner of man he was. It was said that his chains, like St Peter's, were unshackled by angels, or devils; that he could attenuate his body to such a degree that it slid through keyholes; that he could dematerialise himself and pass through solid wood planks and stone walls. In another age, had he wished, he could have become a god for such people, commanding adoration by his performance of miracles. In another age he could have been burnt at the stake.

Chapter Four

DARK WATERS BREAK

Now America wanted him, indeed was clamouring for him. The public there had heard of his remarkable feats, but no one had witnessed them. He had been in Europe for five years. During that time he had visited America twice and only briefly; he had given no performances. At the beginning of 1905, he had received an offer of a six week tour of eastern states for five thousand dollars, but in Europe, with the percentage deal, he was getting over two thousand dollars a week. By the summer, however, he was convinced that the time had come to give Europe a rest. He was offered one thousand dollars a week and when he returned to America it was as a European star.

On 2 October 1905, he opened at the Colonial Theatre, New York, striding onstage to the stirring tune of the 'Kaiser Frederic March', one of his favourite numbers. The escapes the audience saw were the ones he had perfected in Europe. These were enthusiastically received and for the rest of his engagements he played to packed houses. He visited Detroit, Cleveland, Rochester, Buffalo, and in all these cities he was acclaimed. He went on to Washington, where he made headline news when he escaped from the cell which had held Charles J. Guiteau, assassin of President Garfield. Two months later, in Boston, he escaped not only from a cell but from the prison itself, phoning up the reporters who were waiting in the warden's office, still believing him to be securely locked away.

During the next two years he toured all the first class vaudeville theatres in America, meeting all challenges, seemingly escaping from every container ingenuity could devise. As in Europe, he originated most of the challenges himself, but the posters that circulated throughout the towns in which he played always read as though he himself had had no part in the challenge, but was accepting it, as he was bound to accept it, in order to keep his reputation untarnished. He stipulated, however, that the containers must be made to his specifications and delivered to the theatre several days before the escape. They were displayed in the foyer where everyone could examine them, and where, in the secrecy of the night, Houdini could set to work, subjecting the nuts and the bolts, the nails and the cotter-pins, to subtle and invisible change.

He was chary of genuine challenges, not only because he dared leave nothing to chance but also because such challenges tended to be unexciting, lacking the showmanship needed to bring in the crowds. Who else but Houdini could have thought up the series of novel challenge escapes which were to amaze America over the next two years? At Philadelphia, the entire Pennsylvania Football Team, stripped for action, jogged down the aisle of the theatre carrying on their shoulders a giant football. They manacled Houdini and pushed him through the opening of the ball, which was then laced with a brass chain and fastened with a padlock. He escaped in thirty-five minutes. On the stage of Keith's Theatre, Boston, six riveters with blazing torches hammered home the final rivets in an iron boiler. When Houdini entered the boiler, the metal was still hot. Then an iron lid was clanged down into place. The lip of the lid came some inches down the sides of the boiler, and through this lip and the boiler itself two bars of the hardest steel were pushed crosswise and secured with padlocks on the outside. The riveters stood back, convinced that no man could be more firmly contained. The boiler was placed in the cabinet, and the orchestra began to play.

Houdini escaped within an hour, coming through the curtains, sooty and dishevelled.

The audience could only wonder how he had done it, and the more they thought about it the more their wonder grew. They could not know that the impregnable boiler had undergone certain changes while it stood in the foyer of the theatre. The hard steel bars securing the lid had been replaced by bars of soft steel identical in appearance. The genuine steel bars had been hidden in the hollow metal supports of his cabinet. He had escaped by sawing through the soft steel with a tiny saw. Then he retrieved the genuine bars, hiding the fake ones in their place. But to the audience the escape seemed marvellous, miraculous, beyond all rational explanation.

As was the one in Pittsburgh, where he escaped from a sealed glass box, a box with sides of clear glass. The audience could see him inside, trapped and helpless. The box had been thoroughly examined during the days it had stood in the foyer. It was made of single pieces of glass fastened together at the corners by bolts secured with nuts outside the box. The bolt heads inside the box were smooth and could not be unscrewed. Everyone agreed that escape from such a box was impossible. Indeed it was, before Houdini tampered with it, extracting the bolts that fastened the hinges to the corners at the rear of the box, replacing them by bolts with minute indentations on each side of the head, so that with the aid of a tiny crescent of steel he could unscrew the hinge bolts from inside.

He escaped from all kinds of containers, some macabre like a screwed down coffin, some bizarre like a roll-top desk and a piano box. The container did not have to be strong and impenetrable to arouse the interest of the audience. He escaped from a cardboard box and even a paper bag. The audience were intrigued as to how he would get out of the paper bag without tearing it. The bag was seven feet long; he entered it feet first and the flap was pasted down. In the secrecy of his cabinet he cut along the bag with a tiny sharp blade, just below the flap. Once outside the bag he used the blade to cut out another flap, and extracting a tube of paste from one of the hollow supports of the cabinet, fastened the new flap down. The bag was now two or three inches shorter, but no one in the audience thought of measuring it. They were too staggered and dumbfounded.

Whenever possible Houdini escaped from containers not made to his specifications, containers he had not tampered with. The most mysterious of these escapes occurred in Los Angeles, in the autumn of 1907, when he freed himself from a United States government mail bag. The bag was of regulation design; made of heavy canvas and sealed by a leather strap running through a row of metal staples fixed in the collar of the bag. The government secured its mail with great care. The leather strap went over a final staple and was held there by a rotary lock. The only way to escape from the bag was by opening the lock, and as that was on the outside then it was obvious to the audience that escape was impossible.

But attached to Houdini's neck and hidden by his shirt was a long piece of string with a duplicate key tied to the end. There was a small opening at the top of the bag, sufficient for him to push out the key. He held it through the canvas and with fingers made strong through untying knots worked it along the folds until the lock was reached. He opened the lock, escaped, and then fastened it again.

And with this escape, as with all the others, the wonderful thing was that the container did not appear to have been unlocked or tampered with in any way. So in America, as in Europe, it was inevitable that rumours of his supernatural powers should begin to circulate. These became so widespread and persistent that he had to deny them from the stage, emphasising that all his escapes were accomplished by physical means. But with many people these denials only strengthened their belief that this was no ordinary man.

*

And all this time he was thinking up fresh outdoor stunts. These had been originally intended to bring people in to his theatre performances, but more and more the stunts were becoming of greater significance to him. He wanted the whole world to know about him. He was convinced that he had some role to play, but he could not work out what it was. The stunts gave him the chance to be what he had always craved to be—a man whose exploits could not be confined to a theatre but must take place in the great world itself. His jail breaks were losing much of their interest because of imitators, who usually escaped with the collusion of the guards. This infuriated Houdini, for when the public learned of such collusion they naturally assumed that he used the same method. He knew that he must go where imitators would find it hard to follow him, and so he began his famous series of bridge jumps.

The first of these took place on 27 November 1906, in Detroit, when he jumped handcuffed from Belle Isle Bridge and freed himself underwater. This attracted a large crowd, but winter with its freezing temperatures was fast approaching and he had to wait for spring before he could resume his jumps. In May 1907 he leapt, hands and feet manacled, from the bridge at Rochester. His next jump, two weeks later, from Seventh Street Bridge, Pittsburgh, was watched by over forty thousand people.

He was aware that the excitement of the crowd increased the longer he remained under the surface, and so he had a deep bath installed in his home where he practised submerging. By the summer he could hold his breath underwater for an unusually long period. How long is not known; it was probably five or even six minutes, but he himself said that three minutes was his ultimate limit. As always he was leaving nothing to chance, minimising the risk by allowing a margin for error. The jumps were such a hit with the public that he was determined to continue them throughout the winter. So he placed ice blocks in the water of his bath and lay submerged beneath the surface, inuring himself to increasing degrees of coldness.

Unlike the jail breaks and the challenge escapes, these jumps involved risking his life. The thrill for the public lay in the fact that he was overcoming not only the danger of locks but also of water, and if he failed he would die a terrible death by drowning. And where in a flimsy bathing costume could he hide a pick or duplicate key? But Houdini had his methods for all occasions. If he had not already secreted the pick he still had his ways of obtaining it. The jumps were so obviously dangerous that no one thought it anything but fitting that Franz Kukol should step forward at the last minute and give his master a final handshake, yet this was the way by which he passed him the pick. Or what could be more natural than Bess rushing forward to give her husband a fond farewell kiss, yet thereby, while their lips were together, she was able to push the pick into his mouth with her tongue.

In August 1907, in San Francisco, watched by a vast crowd, he made his most thrilling jump. He stood on the parapet of the bridge, high above the dark waters, hands and feet manacled, a seventy-five pound iron ball attached by a chain to his ankle. In his bathing costume his magnificent physique was revealed, developed through constant exercise and strenuous escapes. His chest was deep and broad; his arms were thick and muscular; his calves and thighs bulging and corded. He was thirty-three years old and over the years he had forged his body into a formidable weapon. His teeth could unfasten any knot or buckle. His fingers could work through the heaviest canvas. His feet could do the work of hands. He could survive a long time underwater. He could endure extreme cold. He had disciplined himself to do all these things, and now through the bridge jumps he was learning how to conquer fear. He knew that to do this he needed the utmost repose of the spirit, so that his faculties could work free from mental tension or strain. And that is why those closest to him on the bridge were struck not so much by his physical attributes as by the penetrating clarity of his eyes and the serene, almost mystical tranquillity of his face.

Then holding the heavy ball in his manacled hands he leapt from the bridge, hurtling down and vanishing beneath the water. He was dragged down, down, down to where all was dark as a tomb. There, if he fumbled the release, Death would come for him before coming for his mother. The silent crowd stared down at the water that had closed over his head. One minute passed, then two. It seemed that the worst must have happened, but then the dark waters broke and through them into the daylight came Houdini, alive, hands waving, smiling, and free.

*

He was constantly adding to his repertoire of novel challenge escapes, not only to keep his act fresh but also to keep ahead of his many imitators. It sometimes seemed to him that as fast as he thought up an escape some magician could copy it, crudely perhaps, but sufficient to debase his version. When other magicians actually succeeded in working out one of his methods, he discarded it and thought up some new variation. Then he spoiled their chances by revealing the old method to the public. This happened with the Packing Box Escape, which some magicians had incorporated into their acts. Houdini told his audiences that these deceitful men were able to escape because they had previously hammered out a plank and shortened the nails. To prove that this was not his way, he had his packing case constructed on the stage, plank by plank, using the longest nails. He was able to do this because he had devised a small steel jack, fitted together from two T-shaped lengths of steel, the centre piece of which revolved, forcing the ends outwards. When this was placed in position and twisted, it pushed out the planks no matter how long the nails.

When other magicians had worked out his method of escaping from a screwed down coffin, he revealed to his audience how this was done. He told them that short screws had been substituted for the ones that had secured the bottom of the coffin to the sides. The escape was made by pressing upward against the lid, prising it and the sides away from the bottom. The audience could not know that he was describing the identical method he himself had used. Then he pointed to the coffin from which he was about to escape. Handing screwdrivers to the committee, he encouraged them to remove any screw from the top or the bottom to satisfy themselves that none had been shortened. All the screws inspected were found to be the correct length. Yet he still escaped by raising the top and sides of the coffin away from the bottom, because the screws that secured the bottom had not really been screwed into the sides but into dowels which had been slotted neatly into the sides. So it was not the screws that had been forced out but the dowels with the screws inside them.

So far his never-ending study of techniques had kept him ahead of all his imitators, but ideas for new escapes were not inexhaustible. By the middle of 1907 he realised that he needed some permanent escape; another Metamorphosis, an escape of which the public would never tire. The chief asset of the challenge escape was that the outsiders who manufactured the containers were experts in their field. This guaranteed the authenticity of the container. If, as he believed, the time had come to manufacture his own container, then it must be one from which there seemed to be no possibility of escape; one that the audience could examine and test in any way. And it must be daring, exciting; it must incorporate the double danger of locks and water that made the bridge jumps such a hit with the public. And there must be a challenge. As no one would be challenging him, he would have to issue his own challenge. And who was worthy of that except the greatest adversary of mankind? He would challenge Death.

So he devised the Water Can Escape, which was first featured at the Columbia Theatre, St Louis, on 27 January 1908. A canvas tarpaulin was spread over the floor of the stage, and in the middle of this stood the can. Houdini made his entrance and invited a committee from the audience to step up and inspect the can. They found that it was made of galvanised iron, all seams riveted, and had a metal lid that could be secured by six padlocks. The can stood forty-two inches high and had a sloping shoulder and cylindrical neck; similar in shape to a milk can, but larger, large enough to hold a man.

Houdini announced that the can would be filled with water and he would be placed in it. The committee would lock the lid and hold the keys. The padlocks could be supplied by members of the audience, if any of them so wished. He then went offstage while Franz Kukol supervised a relay of stage-hands carrying buckets of water. When the can was filled Houdini came back on stage, dressed in a bathing costume. He told the audience that man could live but a short time underwater, and that he would first demonstrate how long he himself could remain submerged. He asked them to test how long they could hold their own breath, starting from the instant he went underwater, but he advised those with weak hearts not to try.

Kukol helped to raise him and he entered the can feet first, sliding down, arms raised above his head. The displaced water spilled over the sides and more bucketfuls were added until the can was again brimming full. The audience held their breath, but most were gasping after a minute, and after two minutes everyone had given up. Yet he was still submerged. He remained submerged for three minutes, then he surfaced. He told them that he would now attempt to escape handcuffed from inside the locked can.

A member of the committee handcuffed him, and he slid down inside the can. Other committee members put the metal lid on the can and secured it with the six padlocks. Kukol brought forward the curtained cabinet to conceal the can. A single spotlight played on the front curtain of the cabinet, and the orchestra struck up 'Many Brave Hearts Lie Asleep in the Deep'.

For the first two minutes the audience were not troubled. Houdini had proved that he could stay underwater longer than that. But when the two minutes gave way to three they began to murmur apprehensively. There was a feeling of suspense, of time running out. Another thirty seconds ticked by. The suspense was unbearable. Then Houdini stepped out of the cabinet, dripping water. Behind him stood the can, still locked.

How had he done it? He had escaped by pushing up the top part of the can, separating it from the rest. He was able to do this because the rivets attaching the two parts had been doctored. All he had to do was to push hard and the shoulder, the neck, and the lid, together with the six padlocks, all came away together. Then he put the two parts together and there was the locked can, secure, impregnable.

The Water Can Escape became the climax of his act; it was a sensation wherever he played. He now abandoned the Handcuff Challenge, leaving this to his imitators, although he continued to use handcuffs as part of other escapes. In the spring of 1908, he made a coast to coast tour. He had extended his act from fifteen to thirty minutes. He warmed up with the Strait-Jacket Escape.

He had learned at last how to dramatise this. His brother, Dash, had escaped from a strait-jacket, not in the secrecy of the cabinet, but in full view of the audience. They had been thrilled by the performance. When Houdini heard of this, he too did an escape in front of an audience. They were fascinated by the energy, the sheer brute strength he brought to the struggle. As his fingers beneath the canvas worked on the buckles, they cheered him on, more fervently as each buckle yielded to him. The Strait-Jacket Escape, which he had all but abandoned, became one of his most dramatic routines. He followed it with Metamorphosis (Bess joined him for this), and the Needle Trick. But the presentation of the Water Can Escape, with its building up of tension, took up most of the thirty minutes. The release from that tension never failed to evoke an intense emotional response in his audience. When he emerged from the cabinet, dripping water, they exploded in a thunder of cheers and applause, and it was evident from the joyous atmosphere that filled the theatre that they were not so much acclaiming his achievement as thanking God for his safe deliverance.

*

And all this time he was building up his library on magic; the collection was taking over room after room in his New York home. Whenever he travelled, a crate of books accompanied him, so that he could study even when on tour. That same year, 1908, saw the culmination of his research with the publication of *The Unmasking of Robert-Houdin*. The book was based on a series of articles he had written for the *Conjurer's Monthly Magazine*. He had started this journal almost two years previously, in September 1906, after a quarrel with the editor of the *Sphinx*, the official journal of the Society of American Magicians. On his return from Europe, Houdini had suggested to the editor of the *Sphinx* that he should devote some space to his exploits. The editor said that he would publish any such information at the usual advertising rates; a reply that greatly displeased Houdini. So he started his own journal and wrote most of it himself.

Among the first of his contributions was a series of articles attacking Robert-Houdin. When the series was completed he organised them into a book with the aid of a professional journalist.

The Unmasking of Robert-Houdin added little to the serious study of magic. Scholars had long been aware that Robert-Houdin's claims had been exaggerated, not so much from dishonest motives as from the nature of the man to romanticise. Even so, the book was a considerable achievement for a self-taught man. And Houdini gloried in his new role as author. Two years previously he had published a pamphlet, *The Right Way to Do Wrong*, in which he exposed the methods of pickpockets and other petty criminals. He had written this as a public relations exercise, to show that he was firmly on the side of law and order. He valued his excellent standing with the American police and did not want any of them thinking, as had happened in Germany, that through his prison escapes he was encouraging crime.

But *The Unmasking of Robert-Houdin* was not a pamphlet, it was a book, a real book, with a hard-backed cover, three hundred and nineteen pages of text, and two hundred illustrations. He was delighted with himself. He sent copies to scholars of magic and university professors, pleading almost pathetically in his covering note that they read at least part of the book. He advertised it on posters, in newspapers, from the stage of theatres, and in handbills distributed throughout the streets. These handbills took the characteristic form of a challenge. He challenged the public to read his book and then to find in the whole literature of magic one book that could stand comparison with his.

He now regarded himself not merely as an entertainer but as a writer, a scholar, a serious researcher into all matters concerned with magic and the supernatural. He wondered if perhaps this was the role in life he had been seeking. He was spending most of his income on books and manuscripts, and as his library grew he studied more and more. But no matter how deeply he read the unanswered question still remained, the question he had wanted to put to Alexander Herrmann and Wiljalba Frikell before Death had called on them, closing the door behind him.

Whenever he was in New York, Houdini discussed the question with his friend, Joe Rinn. Could the persistent application of technique break through some barrier, releasing a psychic force which took over from the magician at a critical point of his performance? Joe had made a reputation for himself as an investigator of psychic phenomena, and he related the question to the claims of the spiritualists. He told Houdini that although he had yet to be convinced that their claims were genuine, the attitude taken by some reputable investigators was that while there was a large percentage of fraud in spiritualism there were some authentic psychic phenomena. His friend, David P. Abbott, had written to him of a strange case in West Virginia; a frail, elderly medium, named Mrs Blake, who worked with a trumpet held to her ear. From that trumpet voices came to the listeners, giving details of dead relatives. The case had baffled Abbott. And there was the Italian medium, Eusapia Palladino. Scientists in Italy and France, after subjecting her to numerous tests, had declared her to be a genuine psychic. At the present time she was being investigated by a team that included his friend Hereward Carrington. The investigation was still proceeding, but Carrington had told him that Palladino was producing marvellous phenomena and at no time had the lights in the room been completely extinguished.

Houdini's rational mind was inclined to dismiss all this as nonsense, but his question was still unanswered. He sought out Kellar, America's greatest living magician, for he believed that since the death of Herrmann and Frikell no man knew more about the mysteries of magic. His discussions with Joe Rinn prompted another question. Could this force come to spiritualist mediums because they knowingly and deliberately sought to make contact with it? No one was better placed to answer this question than Kellar. For twenty years he had had a standing challenge to all mediums that he could duplicate their effects. Yet, to Houdini's surprise, he would not come right out and say that spiritualism was all humbug. Then Kellar told him a story, a strange, mysterious story.

During his travels through India in 1882, he had attended

a seance in Calcutta. He went as a sceptic, but had come away utterly unable to explain by any natural means the phenomenon that he had witnessed. The medium, William Eglinton, had ascended into the air and Kellar found himself borne aloft, trying to hold on to him. There was no trace of trickery in any form, nor was there in the room any machinery by which the levitation could have been produced. The mechanical methods by which he had imitated levitation on the stage could not possibly have been used in that room. He told Houdini that despite this experience he remained a sceptic as regards spiritualism, yet he was still unable to account for what must have been a force, which, if his senses were to be relied on, was in no way the result of trickery.

And he told Houdini about the Davenport brothers, the most famous of all stage mediums. He had much to tell, for in his early career he had acted first as their assistant and then as their business manager. Ira and William Davenport had been born in Buffalo, New York, and their phenomena started in the eighteen-fifties, shortly after the manifestations of the Fox sisters, which had caused such an upsurge of interest in spirit communication. The brothers were in their early teens when they produced their first rappings. To test the boys, some observers asked if they would allow themselves to be bound with ropes. The brothers agreed, but when they were tied it seemed that the spirits worked harder for them than before. So it was suggested that they work in a closed cabinet to prevent the possibility of help from confederates in the room. Again they agreed, and devised their famous cabinet.

This was a three-door wooden construction, similar in size and shape to a large wardrobe. In the upper centre of the middle door was an aperture large enough for a hand to pass through. Inside the cabinet two planked seats faced one another. On the floor between stood two handbells and a tambourine. On the wall behind hung a guitar, trumpet, and violin and bow. The brothers were tied to the seats, the doors were closed, and all lights in the room extinguished. Then the musical instruments began to play, the bells rang, and spirit hands appeared through the aperture.

The Davenport brothers went on the stage, and their act was a great success. This was due in no small part to their charming personalities. The boys never claimed supernatural powers, but they travelled with a Unitarian minister, who presented them to the audience and lectured on their performance. The minister believed that everything they accomplished was done with the aid of spirits. The attitude of the Davenports was to leave people to draw their own conclusions, but with a minister as their sponsor, who sincerely believed the phenomena to be caused by spirits, it was inevitable that many in the audience should also become convinced that this was so. It followed that their act did much for the spiritualist cause.

In 1864, after touring America triumphantly for ten years, the Davenports sailed for Europe. In Britain, as in America, they were accepted by many as genuine mediums, and others, while sceptical, admitted being baffled. Rational explanations were put forward. John Nevil Maskelyne, the magician, built a similar cabinet and reproduced all their phenomena. But savants, among them Richard Burton, translator of *The Arabian Nights,* who had travelled widely through the orient and had seen many magicians, believed such explanations to be utterly unreasonable. Even eminent conjurers would not accept Maskelyne's duplication as the true explanation. Spiritualists seized on these comments and publicised them widely. Controversy raged throughout the country —were the Davenports genuine mediums or Yankee tricksters? Feelings ran so high that when the brothers appeared in Liverpool there was a riot, with the audience storming the stage, shouting that the performance was blasphemous. There were similar outbursts in Huddersfield and Leeds, and later in Paris.

The Davenport brothers returned to America in 1868, and Kellar joined them the following year. He believed them to be sincere until he had a friend tie him up in a similar way and found he could release a hand. He left them and started his own act, featuring a similar seance. The Davenports continued their triumphant progress, visiting many countries. Then, in 1877, in Australia, William died. Ira returned heart-broken to America, and retired into obscurity.

Houdini asked Kellar whether he believed any of the Davenports' phenomena could have been the work of spirits. Kellar
said that he did not know but doubted it very much. He admitted
that his own duplication of their effects did not necessarily prove
that they had cheated; and he pointed out that in the twenty-
three years of their public career they had never once been exposed, certainly no record existed of their having been caught
redhanded in a fraud. But he suggested to Houdini that the best
course of action would be to get in touch with Ira Davenport
himself.

Houdini had not realised that, after all these years, Ira Davenport was still alive. He was in fact, to be found at Maysville,
Chautauqua County, New York, living quietly and still sorrow-
ing over his dead brother. Houdini wrote to Ira Davenport, asking
if he might call on him. He wanted to go immediately, but his
commitments would not allow this. For some time Europe had
been demanding him back; he had not been there for three years.
All the arrangements had been made, and he could stay no longer
in America. On 10 August 1908, he sailed with Bess for Germany. The sea was as troubled as his own mind, and on that
unstable element he tossed and rolled in anguish.

Chapter Five

THE THRESHOLD OF DEATH

On 10 September 1908, he began his second European tour at the Circus Busch, in Berlin. In his act he featured Metamorphosis, the Strait-Jacket Escape, the Water Can Escape, and, whenever one could be arranged, a novel challenge escape. This was frequently possible as the escapes of which America had tired were new to Europe, so he escaped from sealed glass boxes, riveted boilers, and paper bags to the utter mystification of his audiences. Europe was seeing him in his prime; thirty-four years old, weighing one hundred and sixty pounds, and in perfect physical condition. He needed to be since his act was the hardest on his body he had ever attempted. He made at least three escapes during his twice-nightly act, a total of six. On the days when he also did matinees the total could be as many as nine.

He seemed determined to push his physical endurance to the utmost limit, for around this time he introduced the Wet Sheet Escape, the most exhausting of all his routines. Like the strait-jacket, the wet sheet treatment was used in lunatic asylums to restrain violent patients. His pre-occupation with it reflected the morbidity of his thoughts. He came onstage dressed in a bathing costume. White robed attendants from the local asylum bound his arms to his sides by winding a piece of cloth round his body and tying it securely. A linen sheet was spread out on the floor of the stage. He lay down on the edge of the sheet and the attendants rolled him up tightly in it. Then he was rolled in another sheet, and another, like a cocoon. He was placed on a bed which had a strong metal frame. Heavy cloth bandages were wound round his ankles, knees, waist, and neck. The ends of the bandages were tied to the bed frame. Four additional bandages were run lengthwise from his head to his feet to make the binding firmer. These also were secured to the bed frame. Then came the part that made the escape so difficult. The sheets were thoroughly soaked with buckets of hot water. This tightened them and made them stick together.

The escape depended on brute strength. He had to worm his way out of the sheets towards the top of the bed. By having his feet fastened first, his body had been drawn down towards the bottom of the bed, which gave him some slack in the top bandages. After an hour and a quarter of intense struggle, he came clear of the sheets and rolled on to the floor. Untying his arms was relatively easy. The escape was never a great success with audiences. Their reaction did not justify the effort involved. Yet he continued to present it, even though afterwards he had barely the strength to walk offstage.

And as if all this were not enough he made many outdoor dives. At Liverpool, weighed down by chains, he jumped into the river Mersey. Sometimes the local authority intervened, fearing his death and the effect this might have on the onlookers. At Dundee, the police refused him permission to jump from the parapet of the lofty Tay Bridge. But he did not disappoint the crowds. He hired a pleasure steamer and dived from that.

It was as though he had taken a vow never to rest. Every moment of his nineteen hour day was filled with activity. He was constantly enlarging his library, shipping crates of books and manuscripts to America. He visited cemeteries, tending the graves of dead magicians. He kept up a vast correspondence. He had instructed Joe Rinn to send him papers and clippings on all psychic matters, and he studied these intently. Wherever he went, he travelled with two thousand pounds of baggage, but only a small percentage of this heavy load was needed for his act. The rest was books and documents that he wanted immediately to hand. Yet he found no answers to the questions that troubled him. Then, in late January 1909, while touring Britain, he received a reply to the letter he had sent to Ira Davenport. The old medium wrote to say that they must meet soon, as there were many things he had to tell him.

Houdini would have returned to America immediately, but he was too heavily booked in Europe. He had another reason for returning; he was pining for his mother. She had looked so frail when he left her. He knew that she could not have many more years of life remaining, and he begrudged every minute spent away from her. His yearning to see her became so great that he could bear it no longer. He wrote to her, begging her to come to England. She came in June, and while she was with him he was content. But by the autumn he had to move on to Germany. He pleaded with her to accompany him, but she told him that she must return home. She reminded him that she had other children, his brothers, Dash, Leopold, Nat, his sister, Gladys. Houdini was playing in Plymouth when her boat was due to sail from Southampton. After the show, he travelled all night through torrential rain to kiss her goodbye.

Never had he been so depressed as during that autumn in Germany. Early in November, when he was playing at Hamburg, he went to the local racetrack, where an aeronaut was to give a demonstration of flying. There he saw his first aeroplane; a fragile construction of wood and white cloth, which looked no more than an enormous box kite. Six years had gone by since Orville Wright had made the first power-driven flight at Kitty Hawk, North Carolina, but aeroplanes were still a great novelty. The aeroplane taxied across the ground, then rose in the air, circled the racetrack and came back to earth. Houdini's spirit was uplifted at the sight. He rushed across the field and questioned the aeronaut about his incredible, beautiful machine. Within a week he possessed his own aeroplane; a Voisin biplane, thirty-three feet six inches in length, powered by a sixty horsepower engine. He also engaged a mechanic from the Voisin workshops to maintain the aeroplane and teach him how to fly.

He soon learned to manipulate the controls. Then came a calm day, a perfect day for flying. He got into the machine and started the engine. The aeroplane bumped across the field, lifted off the ground, and soared through the air. Below him he saw faces craning upwards, the ground streaming out behind them. He saw the black shadow of the aeroplane moving over the green fields. For two minutes he flew in a wide circle, coming back to his starting point. As he approached this, he came gliding down, tilted up the nose at exactly the right moment, levelled again and grounded, as gently as one of the leaves falling on that windless day. His black depression had gone; he was jubilant and exhilarated. He had escaped from the earth, from the pull of gravity. Never in his life had he felt so free.

He could think of nothing but flying, and day after day, whenever the weather allowed, he soared again and again into the sky. But for a time this had to stop. He had accepted an offer to play a short season in Australia. At first he had not been keen, for he had all the work he could handle and the length of the voyage appalled him. But Harry Rickards, an Australian impresario, had flattered his vanity by offering him the highest salary ever paid to an entertainer in Australia. He would receive the full salary while travelling there and back, which meant he would be paid twelve weeks for working and twelve for resting. This was an offer he could not refuse. Moreover, he thought it curiously fitting to be visiting the country where one of the Davenport brothers lay buried.

In January 1910, he sailed from Marseilles. The aeroplane went with him, together with the mechanic. He had learnt that no one had yet flown in Australia, and he was determined to be the first. He was seasick for most of the voyage, and by the time the ship reached Adelaide he had lost twenty-five pounds. Journalists noted that his hair was sprinkled with grey. On 7 February he began an eight week engagement at the New Opera House, Melbourne. As an outdoor stunt, he dived manacled from the Queen's Bridge into the river Yarra, watched by twenty thousand people. When he sank beneath the surface he disturbed a corpse, which floated up beside him, pale and rotten, in the muddy water; a macabre warning that this would probably be the manner of his own death.

All his time away from the theatre was spent with his aeroplane. He had found a field, Digger's Rest, twenty miles from

Melbourne, and there he prepared for his record flight. The weather was against him; day after day the winds blew. He began driving to the field at night, sleeping in the tent beside his aeroplane, and emerging every dawn looking at the sky. He had to wait three weeks for a suitable day. Then, on 16 March, he flew for five minutes, circling the field at fifty miles an hour. His achievement took the country by surprise, and an Aerial League of Australia was hastily organised to present him with a trophy.

At Sydney he visited the grave of William Davenport. The tombstone was decorated with carvings of the cabinet and ropes, but the grave itself was neglected and overgrown. He bought the deeds and arranged for it to be tended in perpetuity. Thoughts of death were with him all the time; only in flying could he find relief from them. Never in the air did he think himself to be in danger; he experienced only peace and contentment. Even when the weather would not allow him to fly, he would go to the field just to be near his aeroplane. He would sometimes get up as early as two in the morning to go out and look at it. By the end of his Australian engagement he was exhausted through lack of sleep. He who had always prided himself on his superb physical condition was losing his energy, his sense of timing. His performances were affected; the risks of failure were increasing. He knew that his obsession with flying must end. He had the aeroplane packed in its crate, and never in his life did he fly again.

*

He sailed across the Pacific Ocean to America and arrived in New York by July, in time for his mother's sixty-ninth birthday. Then he went on to visit Ira Davenport in Chautauqua County, in the south-west corner of New York state. The old medium greeted him warmly and treated him with the deference due to a master. He was touched when Houdini showed him a photograph of his brother's freshly tended grave. Then they sat down to talk. Houdini asked him whether any of their manifestations had been the work of spirits. The old man said that he would tell him all their secrets. They talked throughout the day and far into the night.

Ira Davenport told Houdini that he and his brother had been no more than clever escapologists. All their feats had been accomplished by natural means. Their performances had been so expert that right from the start people believed the manifestations to be supernatural. So they had seen no reason why they should not let their audiences go on believing this. The advantage of working with his brother had been that it was never likely that both of them would be tied so securely as to prevent them doing their act. If one was ever in trouble, the other was ready to come to the rescue. The chance that they could both have been tied at the same time had been a remote one.

But they had always to be on guard against surprise and exposure. Any member of the committee who wanted to go into the cabinet with them had to be tied. This was to immobilise him, although they had told the audience that the reason was to prove beyond doubt that he was not a confederate. They had always reserved the front seats for friends to prevent anyone breaking through. At private sittings they had asked that cord be run through the buttonholes of all present, ostensibly to prevent collusion on anyone's part with either his brother or himself, but really to give protection against surprise seizure. When the controversy over them had been at its height, they had sometimes used as many as ten confederates for protection.

He told Houdini that his brother and he had never claimed supernatural powers. Houdini knew this to be true, but he also knew that they had allowed others to claim them on their behalf. There had been the Rev J. B. Ferguson, the Unitarian minister, who had travelled with them, and later, Thomas L. Nicholls. They had believed that everything accomplished by the brothers had been the work of spirits. The old man agreed that this was so, and that neither of their sponsors had ever been disillusioned since they had never been told the secrets of the manifestations. His brother and he had allowed them to make their own comments, thinking it better showmanship to leave the audience to draw their own conclusions. He admitted that having the act presented by a minister who sincerely believed the phenomena to be genuine must have led many people to reach a similar belief. But had they presented their act as a conjuring trick it would not have aroused such curiosity or earned them so much money. Their parents had died believing them to have supernatural powers. He and his brother had not dared to confess to them the true nature of their work, fearing what the shock of disillusionment might do.

Houdini travelled home, perturbed. True, Ira Davenport had denied that either his brother or himself had supernatural powers. He had said repeatedly that neither of them were mediums. Yet they had allowed their sponsors to go on believing that they were genuine. If they were fakes, then their continued silence in the matter was manifestly a lie. And not only a lie but a blasphemy, for their act had been presented in a religious context. At the same time he had been impressed by the goodness of the old man. It seemed inconceivable that he would have allowed his father and mother to go to their grave believing something untrue about him, or to have had the cabinet and ropes carved on his brother's tombstone if these had indeed been the symbols of deceit and trickery. Houdini doubted that Ira Davenport had told him all his secrets, and he resolved to visit the old man again as soon as possible.

He stayed in America less than a month, for he had to return to Europe to continue the tour interrupted by his trip to Australia. In Britain he found that the imitators had been busy and the Water Can Escape was being done by other magicians. He immediately introduced a variation by having an iron-bound chest built and escaping from the locked can inside the locked chest. And to discredit those who were performing the handcuff act he himself had discarded, he published *Handcuff Secrets*, in which he exposed the methods they used.

But to keep ahead he knew he must invent an escape even more sensational than the Water Can. Since changing from handcuffs and jailbreaks to escapes which depended more on mechanical construction, he had felt the need for some expert assistance. Franz Kukol was indispensable, but he was no mechanic. Houdini needed someone who could take his rough sketches and develop them into working plans. While in Britain, he found such a man in James Collins.

James Collins was to prove a great asset to Houdini. He was a master mechanic, expert joiner, and metal worker. Yet no one looked more ordinary or inconspicuous, a 'typical' British working man; and as such he was often to pass as a member of the committee from the audience. He was also utterly calm and dependable. No crisis on stage or off could upset him.

During this same visit Houdini took on a third assistant, James Vickery, employed for general duties, although being a man of stolid upright appearance he would sometimes come onstage whenever a plain clothes detective, hospital attendant, or some other official looking character was needed for the act. Kukol was still the chief assistant, completely in charge in the theatre, handling the stage-hands and arranging the music. But for Houdini Collins was now the most important, and his first task was to construct an escape to take the place of the Water Can.

Houdini already had the basic idea of this escape. Together Collins and he worked on the detailed drawings. Then they ordered the various parts from different workshops to preserve secrecy. Bit by bit the construction was pieced together until it was finally assembled. Houdini tested it, and then had it crated and stored in London. There it would remain until needed.

In the meantime he went on with his act, extending his repertoire of challenge escapes whenever possible. In February 1911, in the town square of Chatham, he was strapped and chained to the mouth of a cannon, then a fifteen minute time fuse was inserted. He escaped in six minutes. And he continued his variations of the Water Can Escape. He had the can filled with milk to prove that his escape owed nothing to his ability to see through water. In Leeds he had the can filled with beer, but while being locked in he was overcome by the fumes, and Kukol had to rescue him. This miscalculation worried Houdini. His career depended on never making such a mistake.

By the summer he was back in America, anxious to talk again

with Ira Davenport. He wrote asking when he might visit him. On 8 July Ira Davenport was waiting for Houdini to come, but as with Wiljalba Frikell, Death came before him.

*

In the autumn Houdini began a tour of the eastern states. The American public had not seen him for three years. The challenge escapes he had devised in Europe were new to them, and he never neglected an opportunity to enlarge his repertoire. While playing in Boston, the newspapers were full of reports of a strange sea monster brought ashore by Cape Cod fishermen. It was described as a cross between a whale and an octopus. Houdini arranged for the Lieutenant Governor of Massachusetts to challenge him to escape Jonah-like from its belly. The monster was brought to the theatre and Houdini, shackled hand and foot, was forced through a slit in its side, which was then laced up with a heavy chain. More chains were wound round the carcass and fastened with locks. The curtained cabinet was brought forward to enclose the monster, the orchestra began to play, and the audience waited. They did not know that Houdini, gasping and choking, was fighting for his life. Taxidermists had treated the monster internally with an arsenic solution in order to preserve it and the acrid fumes were suffocating him. Kukol, listening outside the cabinet, believed his master was giving distress signals, then, just as he was about to investigate, Houdini emerged, free. But again an escape had gone wrong; he had failed to calculate all the risks.

In November, in Detroit, after escaping from a challenge bag, he suffered sharp pains in his groin and began passing blood. He continued his tour, but three weeks later, in Pittsburgh, he was worse. He consulted a doctor, who diagnosed a ruptured blood vessel in one of the kidneys, and advised complete rest for some months and the abandonment for ever of all strenuous escapes. Houdini rested for two weeks, but in December he was back on the road again. Far from abandoning the strenuous escapes he was performing them more frequently. He even continued with

Houdini. '... stocky and slightly bow-legged, the face finely formed, the expression serious and proud.'

Houdini's father

Alexander Herrmann. 'Never for a moment, whether on stage or off, did Herrmann the Great cease to be a magician'

Jean-Eugène Robert Houdon. '. . . the great magician, before whom he would bow his head or even kneel in homage'

KELLAR

LEVITATION

Kellar's famous illusion, 'Levitation of Princess Karnac.' '... he claimed
... that he had seen Fakir miracles at the courts of Mohammedan rahahs,
and battled through high Himalayan snows to witness levitations in
Tibetan lamaseries'

Katie Fox gets an answer from
the spirits. 'Jo believes this was
the time of a new Revelation,
a new Pentecost ...'

Houdini and Bess performing Metamorphosis. 'His expression was grave, and to many people in the audience his powerful head, wide brow and aquiline nose suggested the bust of a Roman consul or general

Early publicity photograph. 'A man, naked against the world, bound in chains, deprived of all help . . .'

Poster for the Water Can Escape
'. . . the double danger of lock
and water'

Houdini about to perform the
Water Can Escape. 'He would
challenge Death'

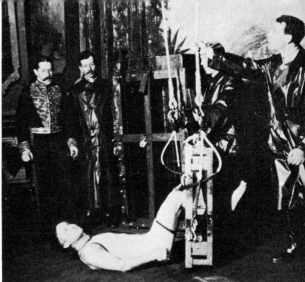

Bridge jump. 'Then holding the heavy ball in his manacled hands he leapt from the bridge, hurtling down and vanishing beneath the water'

Stage 1 of the Chinese Water Torture Cell Escape

Houdini performing the Upside-Down Strait-Jacket Escape. 'They saw the strait-jacket slipping down over his chest and over his head. Then the final moment of triumph when discarded it fell to the ground'

Preparing to be submerged in the swimming pool of the Shelton Hotel. 'If I die it will be the will of God and my own foolishness'

'. . . he was never to adapt himself to a separate existence from
his mother'

Houdini and Bess.
'Rosabelle, Sweet Rosabelle,
I love you more than I can
tell . . .'

Genii
The Conjurors Magazine
Vol. 26 · October, 1961 · No. 2 · 50c

Houdini and Sir Arthur Conan Doyle.
'At first sight they seem an incongruous pair . . . the tall patrician Englishman and the stocky self-made Jew'

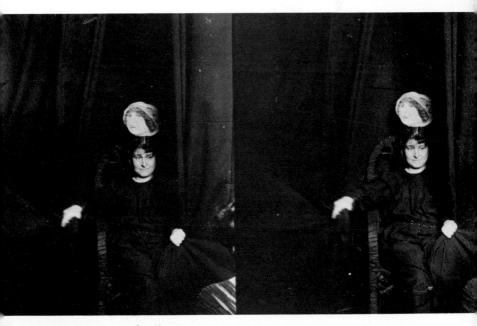

Eva C. with whom he sat five times.
'Through Doyle Houdini now had introductions to the best mediums in the land'

Mina Crandon, 'Margery the Medium'.
'She was very attractive; a natural blonde with blue eyes, infectious laugh and a marvellous figure'

Houdini duplicating Marge phenomena. 'Margery had be exposed. Houdini left no one doubt about that'

the Wet Sheet Escape, physically the most difficult, wrenching as it did every muscle in his body.

Early in 1912, while performing this escape, he tore a ligament in his side. The pain lasted several weeks, and the pain from his damaged kidney was continuous. Little as he usually slept, he was now hardly sleeping at all. He lay in bed with a pillow under his side to relieve the pressure on his kidney. He also wore a black silk bandage over his eyes, for should he succeed in falling asleep the least ray of light awakened him. Yet he continued with the strenuous escapes. It was as though he had to torture his body in order to alleviate the torment of his mind. More and more the thought of his mother's death troubled him. He knew that this could not be long delayed, and so he forced his pain-racked body not only through the theatre routines but also the bridge jumps and other outdoor stunts. These stunts were becoming more dangerous as his mother aged and sickened.

For he was preparing to go where no imitators could follow him. With a fierce logic he was carrying his escapes to the very border between life and death. Thoughts of coffins, tombstones, and skeletons had been with him all his life. In his escapes he was symbolically buried and reborn, acting out mankind's age-old belief in death and resurrection—the rebirth of the sun and the seasons, the grief of Good Friday and the joy of Easter Sunday. It could be that death was a negative thing leading only to the melancholy decomposition of the grave, or it could be that man must die in the dark to find rebirth in the light. In that event, death was the ultimate escape, and the supreme trick of the magician would be to enter the world beyond, if only for a flickering second, and then return.

During July and August 1912, he appeared at Hammerstein's Roof Garden, New York. To coincide with his opening, he performed the most dangerous outdoor stunt he had yet attempted. Handbills and newspapers told the city that on Sunday, 7 July, he would be nailed in a box and thrown from Pier 6 into the East River. He would then attempt to release himself while the box was submerged. On the day a great crowd assembled, but the police would not allow him to operate from the pier. So he hired a tug and together with a party of reporters steamed out to the open harbour. His brother Dr Leopold Weiss came along in case his medical services were needed.

The New York reporters had always been cool towards Houdini's achievements, but on this day even they were impressed by his brink-of-death intensity. They manacled him, put him in the packing case and nailed down the lid. The sealed box was roped, circled with steel bands, and weighed down with two hundred pounds of iron lashed to its sides. Then the box was lowered down a chute into the sea. It sank immediately. The reporters looked down to where the box had vanished, then shouted with amazement as Houdini surfaced fifteen feet away. The box was hauled aboard and examined by the reporters. They found the nails, ropes, and steel bands all in place. They prised off the lid and there inside were the manacles, still locked. Later that summer he performed yet another dangerous outdoor stunt. He had himself roped at the highest point of the Heidelberg Building Tower and then hung out into space three hundred feet above Broadway. Then he escaped, watched by great crowds on the sidewalks below.

In the early autumn, he set off on a European tour. He paused briefly in London to take out of storage the new feature escape that was to replace the Water Can, then went on to Germany, to Bremen, where he had an engagement with the Circus Busch. There he planned to escape for the first time from the Chinese Water Torture Cell. This was the greatest escape he ever made. More than anything he did, this was for many people the conclusive proof that he had supernatural power. Even today the secret of the escape is not known for certain.

He strode on to the stage and bowed to the cheering audience. He seemed older than they remembered him; hair greying, face thinned by pain, a tighter line to the mouth. They noted the nobility of the head, the confident carriage, the suggestion of greatness, and they were thrilled at the sight of him. There was an electric feeling in the air. This was the hero who took on all odds single-handed. And tonight, as he was telling them, he would attempt his most dangerous escape.

He pointed to the Cell, a metal-lined mahogany tank with a plate glass front, and he explained its construction. He told them that the glass front was necessary in case he was overcome or his nerve failed him. They would not want him to drown, would they, to make a holiday? No! No! they shouted, Oh no! Then if he were in difficulties, his assistants would smash the glass and do their best to save him. And that was why a metal cage would be inserted in the Cell, to prevent the rushing out of water dashing his body against the broken glass.

He invited a committee of the audience to step on to the stage. He allowed them to make a detailed inspection of the apparatus. When they pronounced themselves satisfied, the Cell was filled with water. While this was being done, he went off-stage to change into a bathing costume. When he returned, he stretched himself out on the floor. His ankles were secured in wooden stocks with metal bindings, which were held in place by a massive frame. This was hauled aloft until he hung head down above the Cell. He took some deep breaths, then clapped his hands as a signal to be lowered into the Cell. When this was done, the frame that held the stocks formed the top of the Cell. A metal grille was clamped over this, hasps were snapped up and padlocks fastened through them. All this was done by members of the committee. The audience could now see him through the glass front. He was underwater, hanging upside down, ankles gripped, trapped and helpless. The Cell was then covered by a curtained cabinet. Franz Kukol and James Collins stood on the alert outside, dressed in firemen's helmets, long black raincoats, rubber boots, and carrying axes.

The orchestra began to play. One minute went by, then two. The audience were tense. Two and a half minutes. Three. There were murmurs of alarm. As with the Water Can, there was the feeling of time running out, but the danger now was incomparably greater. He was not only sealed under water, he was clamped in stocks, upside down. The sheer helplessness of his position was appalling. Some people were becoming hysterical. Houdini must surely be drowning if not already dead. Franz Kukol and Collins looked restless and anxious. They stood close to the

D

cabinet, listening. There were shouts that Houdini should be rescued. Kukol and Collins raised their axes, and at that very moment Houdini appeared, drawing aside the curtain. He stood there dripping water, eyes bloodshot, specks of foam on his lips. Behind him was the Cell, empty and intact, as strongly locked as before. The audience exploded in an outburst of relief and joy, touched with awe. He had drawn aside the curtains of the cabinet as though from the mouth of a tomb, as though, like Lazarus, he had come back from the dead.

In the summer of 1913, he returned to America. He had broken his European tour to play a two week engagement at Hammerstein's Roof Garden. He had accepted this chiefly because it would give him the only chance to see his mother that year. She was now seventy-two years old and very feeble. The Chinese Water Torture Cell Escape created a sensation.

On 8 July he sailed for Europe to resume his tour. His mother saw him off at the pier. He clung to her, hugging and kissing her. Then he went up the gang plank, but returned to embrace her again. He could not bring himself to leave her, and eventually she had to push him gently away. As the ship left the pier, he threw her a paper streamer. She caught it and it tightened between them. He leaned out over the prow, holding the streamer as long as he could. Then he had to let it slip through his fingers, and it flickered down through the sunlight to the waters below. Nine days later, at the Circus Beketow, in Copenhagen, he was handed a cablegram. He read it and fell unconscious to the floor. His mother was dead.

Part Two

Legerdemayne now helpith me right nought.
Farewell my craft and all such sapience,
For Deth hath more maistries than I have wrought.

Lines addressed to Death by John Rekyll,
Court Magician to King Henry V. From
'The Dance of Death' painted in the
north cloister of Old St Paul's Church,
London, in the reign of Henry VI.

Chapter Six

THE UNKNOWN MESSAGE

He was taken to his hotel in great pain; the shock had brought
on his kidney trouble. He was very ill, but he was determined
to travel home immediately. He cabled Dash to delay the funeral,
and then he travelled to Bremen to catch the first available boat.
He arrived in New York on 29 July, and went straight to the
house and into the room where his mother lay. He knelt beside
her body and placed his ear to her heart, as he had so often done
since childhood. But there was nothing for him to hear, no
sturdy beat to reassure him. The following day she was buried
beside her husband in the family plot Houdini had purchased.
When she had said goodbye to him on the pier, he had asked
what present he should bring her back from Europe. She had
asked for a pair of warm woollen slippers. He had bought these
in Bremen on his return journey, and he placed them beside her
in the coffin.

Dash and his sister, Gladys, gave him all the details of their
mother's last hours. A fortnight previously she had been stricken
with paralysis. The following night, as they sat by her bedside,
she kept trying to give them some message for Houdini. She tried
desperately to tell them, but she could not get the words out and
eventually she closed her eyes, exhausted. She died at fifteen
minutes past midnight.

Houdini believed that the message had to do with a family
crisis which had arisen shortly before his departure for Europe; a
terrible blow which his mother had tried to save him from knowing until he returned, and she herself had resolved the matter in

her own mind. Sadie, the wife of his brother, Nat, had left her husband to marry another brother, Leopold. The rest of the family regarded this as a dreadful sin. Houdini loved Leopold, but he could not bring himself to forgive him. He had told his mother that in this matter he would be guided by her, but now she had died before she could tell him what to do.

Had his mother been asking him to forgive his brother? He questioned Dash and Gladys over and over again, but they could only repeat what they had already told him; that his mother had been too weak, too paralysed to speak distinctly. The only word they were able to work out had been his own name. What had she tried to say? He asked himself the question over and over again, but no answer came. He could never know whether the message contained the word, FORGIVE, the one word she would want to send, the one word he would want to hear. He had been denied the last words his mother had wished to speak at that most awful and solemn of moments, the time when the immortal soul is preparing to leave the human body. What had she tried to say? The mystery drove him frantic. He was grief-stricken enough as it was and guilt-ridden that he had not been present when his mother died. Now he was faced with a mystery that he could never solve.

He visited his mother's grave every day and also every night at fifteen minutes past midnight, the instant of her death. He lay flat on the ground, his arms embracing her grave, his face pressed close to the earth. There he talked to her, begging her to let him know her last words. He had always feared that her death would drive him insane. He now believed that this would surely happen unless he solved this mystery. His work was forgotten. His time was spent at her grave or in other activities associated with her memory. He gathered together all the letters she had ever written to him. As he read them again he wept. It seemed to him that each one was a love story, a prayer to God to protect him, a plea that he should always be good. Messages of sympathy poured in from his friends, and in his acknowledgments he exhorted them to cherish their mothers, if still alive.

Through the night Bess heard him calling out his mother's

name again and again. She would put her arms about him and
console him. Over the years he had tended to take her for
granted; in many ways she had taken second place to his mother.
Now she had become both wife and mother. She nursed him in
her arms and reminded him of the happy times they had spent
together since their first meeting at Coney Island, where they
had both appeared on the same bill, he as one of the Houdini
Brothers and she as one of the Floral Sisters. She and her partner
had sung a song, a song that had been all the rage that summer.
She sang it to him now.

> Rosabelle, sweet Rosabelle,
> I love you more than I can tell;
> O'er me you cast a spell,
> I love you, my Rosabelle.

It was his favourite song. He had had the words engraved on
the inside of her wedding ring, and he had kept singing the song
to her throughout their life together. And so Bess brought him
to some semblance of normality, and at the end of August he
was able to resume his European tour. His last act before leaving
New York was to pray beside his mother's grave.

In September and October he toured Germany, and during
November he played in Paris. His act, featuring the Torture
Cell, was a sensational success. The applause gratified him, but
the instant the curtain descended his grief surged back. At the
end of the Paris engagement, Bess took him for a short holiday
to Monte Carlo in the hope that some gambling might distract
him. But even in that bright pleasure resort he remained melancholy and dispirited. The only place that interested him was the
graveyard. There he was drawn to the section where the suicides
were buried; those who had lost all their money at the gaming
tables. Bess tried to force his mind into livelier channels, suggest-
ing visits to the casino and the theatre, but he preferred to
wander among the tombstones. She was disturbed when he
pointed out to her the grave of a husband and wife who had
committed suicide together.

It was the same in London, which he visited for the Christmas
season. His days were spent among the dead. Even his business

stationery now had a black mourning border, and when the Magicians' Club gave a dinner in his honour his pre-occupations
found expression in his speech of thanks. His fellow-magicians
listened, sympathetic but embarrassed, while he told them that
his mother had been everything to him, that not until she had
been taken from him had he realised how futile was man's intel-
ligence when face to face with Death. Bess believed that he was
never the same man after the death of his mother; the old
vitality had gone.

But he had to continue working. Although he had earned a
lot of money in his time he had no savings. His mania for collecting was the chief cause; also he was a most generous man.
Anyone with a hard-up story was likely to get a hand-out, especially if they were connected with magic. To some impoverished
magicians he paid a regular pension. Unlike the ballyhoo that
accompanied his public exploits, his charitable activities were
done so secretly that it was not until after his death that the full
measure of his generosity was known. He was almost forty years
old. He knew that he could not go on doing strenuous escapes
for the rest of his life. So, in England, he organised a full-scale
magic show.

'The Magical Revue' opened in mid-April 1914. Cards vanished from his finger-tips. He plucked gold and silver coins out
of the air until he had a bucketful. A beautiful girl vanished
from the centre of the stage and another one appeared in her
place. It was a good show, but not what audiences expected from
Houdini. To them his name did not mean sleight-of-hand and
illusion, but the fearless challenger shaking a defiant fist at
Death. Houdini was aware of this, but how long could he continue his escapes? Although his spirit was willing, his strained
ligaments and damaged kidney were a constant reminder that
his flesh was not.

But his ability to amaze remained unabated. Towards the end
of June Bess and he travelled home on the *Imperator*. Ex-Presi-
dent Theodore Roosevelt was also a passenger. At the ship's
concert Houdini conducted a mock seance. He asked for questions
to be written on pieces of paper. These would be collected in a

basket and then one of them, chosen at random, would be submitted to his spirit guide, who would write the answer on a slate.
The passengers wrote down their questions, folded their pieces of
paper and waited for the basket to come round. Then Houdini
had a sudden inspiration and changed the routine. He asked
Roosevelt to place his question personally between two blank
slates. Roosevelt did this, and Houdini closed the slates together.
When the slates were opened, Roosevelt saw on one of them a
map in coloured chalk of an area in South America with an arrow
indicating a point on the River of Doubt. The question he had
asked was 'Where did I spent last Christmas?', and on the map
the arrow pointed to the very spot.

Roosevelt was baffled and to many in the audience it seemed a
true manifestation of the supernatural. The news spread from the
elegant passengers in the first class lounge down to the deepest
bowels of the ship, where half-naked stokers, bathed in a red
glow, fed the giant furnaces. Passengers and crew were conscious
that they carried with them an extraordinary man. The wireless
operator tapped out the details of the miracle to New York, and
the story was headline news before the ship reached America.

And yet the explanation was simple enough. Houdini had
known in London that Theodore Roosevelt would be travelling
home on the same boat. He also knew that Roosevelt had written
a series of articles on his South American expedition which were
appearing in the *Daily Telegraph*. With the connivance of a
reporter friend, he had seen some of the articles not yet published.
One of these was illustrated with a map, which he had copied.
At the start of his mock seance he had suggested 'Where did I
spend last Christmas?' as a possible question for the spirit guide.
He had ready the prepared question 'Where did Theodore Roosevelt spend last Christmas?'. This he would have chosen apparently
at random, if necessary.

Yet he still wanted to know whether his suggested question
had been taken up by Roosevelt. As Roosevelt prepared to write
down his question, Houdini picked up a book from a nearby
table and thoughtfully handed it to him to act as a support. He
had previously placed under the dust wrapper a sheet of writing

paper topped by a carbon. When he retrieved the book, he palmed the sheet of paper and discovered that Roosevelt had indeed written the desired question. At this juncture he dramatically changed his routine, asking Roosevelt to place his question personally between the slates. Whichever way things had gone the trick would have been baffling, but giving Roosevelt the answer to his own direct question added tremendously to its impact.

The feat aroused high expectations among his American public, and they were not to be disappointed. On 9 July he opened for his third successive season at Hammerstein's Roof Garden, and during the second week he walked through a solid brick wall. The wall was built onstage by a gang of bricklayers; a real wall of bricks and mortar, ten feet long and nine feet high. It was built on a steel beam, a foot wide and ten feet long, mounted on castors which raised it three inches from the floor. When the wall was completed, Houdini called for a round of applause for the bricklayers, who then left the stage. The wall was inspected by a committee from the audience; they could find nothing false about it.

Houdini announced that he would now walk through the wall. To allay suspicions that he would use a trap-door, a rug was spread on the stage and over this an even larger square of seamless muslin. The wall was then rolled into position over the centre of the muslin, with one end turned towards the audience so that they could see both sides clearly. The committee circled the wall; some stood on the edges of the muslin to prevent any trickery with the floor. A three-fold screen, six feet high, was set against one side of the wall and a similar screen against the other. These did not in any way cover the wall.

He entered the left hand screen and closed it around him. He was hidden from sight, but he raised his hands above the screen and called out 'Here I am.' His hands vanished and a few seconds later appeared above the screen on the other side of the wall, as he called out 'Now I'm here.' Then he pulled back the screen to reveal himself. The audience were too startled to applaud. It had been impossible for him to go over, around or under the wall, which meant that he must really have walked through it. But solid mass could not pass through solid mass, unless, unless . . . No wonder the belief was gaining ground that this man could dematerialise his body.

Yet it was just a trick, an idea he had bought in England. The trick in its original form was to walk through a sheet of steel, but Houdini with his flair for showmanship had altered this to a brick wall, so that the audience could watch its construction on stage. And he had used a trap-door. The rug and the muslin sheet were masterpieces of misdirection. When Houdini stepped behind the screen, Collins, below stage, opened a trap-door. The rug sagged under the weight of Houdini's body sufficiently for him to wriggle under the beam that supported the wall. The members of the committee, who stood on the edges of the muslin were unwittingly assisting him. Their weight kept the muslin taut, so that the sag in the carpet beneath it was not noticeable.

*

Professionally Houdini was riding high, but the following month his career was drastically affected by the outbreak of the First World War. At a stroke he was deprived of his European public. Britain, France, and Germany were at war. Britain and Germany had been the scenes of his greatest triumphs. He was more popular there even than in his own country. In the fourteen years that had elapsed since sailing unknown for England he had spent more than half the time in Europe. It was as a European star that he had conquered America. Now all was changed and the first sign of this was saying goodbye to Franz Kukol, who was returning to Austria to rejoin his regiment. It was a sad parting for both of them.

Houdini knew that for the duration of the war he would need to concentrate on American tours. Before leaving New York he visited his mother's grave, as he had done every day since returning from England. He lay stretched out, his cheek against the ground, and whispered to her in the cold earth below. He told her all the things that had happened to him since his last visit and, as always, he begged her to give him some indication of what she had tried to tell him on her death bed. Had it to do with Leopold's sinful action? Did she want him to forgive his brother? He could not bring himself to do this unless she told him to. He had always done as she asked. But no answer came and he left the graveyard, desolate.

He set off on tour with the question still tormenting him. He feared that if he did not solve the mystery of his mother's last message then he would surely go out of his mind. Wherever he played he visited the local lunatic asylum, morbidly convinced that he would end his days in one. From this dread came the idea for a new outdoor stunt, strenuous and dangerous enough to allow him to battle physically at least against the dark forces that raged inside his head.

He was strapped in a strait-jacket and taken to the top of the highest building in the town, where stood a crane with a hanging rope, stark against the sky, sinister as a gallows. He was secured by his ankles to the end of the rope and swung out head downwards over the street, his body turning dizzily. There, watched by a huge crowd, he began his escape. It was a thrilling experience for them. The excitement lay in the high altitude, the helplessness of his position, his violent contortions, the twisting and arching of his body. They saw the strait-jacket slipping down over his chest and over his head. Then the final moment of triumph when discarded it fell to the ground. His hands were waving and the crowd waved back, delighted. But his own exhilaration did not last long. The very success of the stunt intensified his fears, bringing with it a terrifying question. If he should be incarcerated in a lunatic asylum, he who could escape from strait-jackets and locked cells, then how would they restrain him in his madness?

Over the next two years the stunt brought him much publicity. In Washington he escaped from the top of the Munsey building in view of the biggest crowd ever assembled in the city except for the inauguration of a President. In Baltimore fifty thousand spectators jammed Baltimore and Charles Street while he hung from the cornice of the *Sun* building. Police estimated the crowd as the biggest ever seen in the streets since the Great Baltimore Fire of 1904. The stunt was physically exhausting, but he persisted with it not only because it was such a crowd-puller but also because of the relief it brought to the tension in his mind. In 1916 he prepared himself for another outdoor stunt, even more strenuous, and even more suited to his pre-occupations. He planned to have himself buried alive in the earth.

In a field near Santa Ana, California, Collins and Vickery dug a grave six feet deep. Houdini jumped in and crouched face downwards on his hands and knees, covering his head with a hood. His assistants began to shovel the earth on top of him. He had hoped that the space made by his arched body would provide him with sufficient air to claw his way upwards. But the grave was barely half filled before the earth was clogging his mouth and nose. He tried to call for help, but neither Collins nor Vickery could hear him and they continued filling in the grave. The soil was pressing him down. Desperately he tore his way upwards. His assistants saw two clawing hands appear above the surface of the grave. They grabbed them and hauled him to safety. He had misjudged the killing weight of the earth and so he abandoned the stunt. But he was still obsessed with burial and the week before Christmas in Salt Lake City, he escaped from a coffin which had been sealed inside a steel tomb.

Was his mother in the earth, in the coffin? Her corrupting body certainly, but was she somewhere else? He prayed that she might come back from wherever she was and console him, if only for a moment. In the night Bess would waken and hear him say, 'Mama, are you here?' Then sadly he would fall back on his pillow. He had thought she had come, but she had not. He wondered if he could get in touch with her. The only people who believed this was possible were the spiritualists, but in his opinion all mediums were fakes, dishonest magicians preying on the grief of bereaved people. He had become one himself for a short time in his early career and the episode still troubled his conscience. Together with Joe Rinn he had investigated psychic phenomena, but he had witnesed nothing that he could not have duplicated himself by natural means.

Yet the mediums were the only people who claimed that they could bring his mother back to him. So he forced himself to keep an open mind on a subject he had previously dismissed as hocus-pocus; to be favourably disposed towards those whom he had always believed to be spook crooks. But his need to contact his mother overrode his rational judgment and he swore that if a genuine medium existed he would search the world until he found him.

So his strange quest began. He attended seances, sitting with the same rapt hungry look that had troubled his conscience when he had seen it on the faces of his clients. Now he was as anxious for a message as they had been. Bess tells us that even after numerous disappointments, whenever they visited a new medium, he would close his eyes and join fervently in the opening hymn. So the seance would go on with the same trivial messages and the usual spook tricks he could have done himself with his hands tied behind his back. The rapt look faded from his face and Bess's heart ached for him. She was sometimes tempted to give the medium the one word he longed to hear, the word FORGIVE. But she could not betray his trust, and through the night she would hear him whisper, 'Mama, I have not heard.'

In 1917 America entered the war. At forty-three Houdini was too old to enlist; a further reminder that he was no longer a young man. His act, featuring Metamorphosis and the Torture Cell, was strenuous. In addition, he was frequently performing the Upside-Down Strait-Jacket Escape. He knew that he could not keep up this pace much longer. But what was he to do? The full-scale magic show would be the best field to move into, even though he would be competing with Thurston, the master of stage magic. It was not in his nature to be second to any man. He believed the time had come for Thurston to be made aware that his pre-eminent position was being challenged. Houdini had added to the history of stage magic by walking through a brick wall. To top this he knew that he must do something really big, and big is the only word to describe the trick he performed when he caused an elephant to vanish from the stage of the New York Hippodrome.

Magicians had made doves, rabbits, and even horses disappear, but never an elephant, the largest of all land animals. Houdini did this for the first time on 7 January 1918. A huge wooden cabinet brightly painted in many colours filled the centre of the stage. The elephant, led by its trainer, was marched round the cabinet. Then Houdini announced that he would make it vanish into thin air. The elephant was led into the cabinet, and the curtains closed. When these were opened the elephant had disappeared; the whole solid mass which had lumbered so heavily across the stage was gone. Where it had been there was nothing, nothing but empty space.

Even magicians were confounded by the trick, for they knew that there was no trap-door in the floor of the Hippodrome. Some said that the back wall of the cabinet was really a pair of hinged doors, through which the elephant had been led into a smaller cabinet. But the trick had been performed fifteen feet from the backdrop and the elephant had been marched all the way round the cabinet, thus proving that there was space behind. Others said that the elephant was still in the cabinet, but could not be seen because the bright colours in which the cabinet was painted created an optical illusion. Nobody knew for certain how the trick was done, but as Houdini remarked, they were in good company, for not even the elephant knew. That same season he brought the Needles Trick to its highest state of perfection when he pulled two hundred threaded needles out of his mouth and draped them across the vast stage of the Hippodrome. He boasted that with the elephant and the needle he had presented the largest and smallest tricks in the history of magic.

*

So he continued to enlarge his repertoire of tricks against the day when he would need to fall back on a full-scale magic show. Then an alternative career presented itself. After the Hippodrome season he starred in a movie serial. Silent serials, unlike the later talkie serials, were made for adults as well as children. They were important to the growth of the movie industry, since they enticed audiences to return week after week. These serials were a combination of suspense, action, and romance. At times the audience had difficulty in accepting the heroics performed by serial stars, so some producers had begun to cast real life heroes, men who essentially played themselves. After Houdini, James J. Corbett was to star in a serial about boxing, as was Jack Dempsey, and later Gene Tunney. Houdini was engaged by Octagon Films Incorporated to star in a fifteen chapter silent serial, *The Master Mystery*, to be filmed at Yonkers, New York. He was pleased to accept. He regarded the venture as a new challenge. He was fascinated by every aspect of the production, and insisted on lending a hand with the script.

He played Quentin Locke, undercover agent for the Department of Justice, investigating International Patents Inc., a vast organisation controlled by an evil tycoon, who stopped all progress likely to ruin his business interests. This organisation was run from a castle fortress. Beneath the castle, in deep caves carved from solid rock, was The Graveyard of Genius, filled with prototypes of futuristic machines purchased from their inventors but destined never to be used. The most powerful agent of the organisation was Q the Automaton, a robot with a human brain. Q appeared in every episode, smashing its way through all obstacles to get Quentin Locke, who was usually occupied freeing himself from other predicaments—strait-jackets, manacles, and ropes. He was bound to the bottom of an elevator shaft as the car inched down to crush him. He was nailed in a packing case and tossed into the sea. He escaped from an electric chair, and from a coil of barbed wire as a stream of acid flowed towards him.

The serial was moderately successful and another company, Paramount-Artcraft, signed him up for two full-length feature films. The first of these, *The Grim Game,* was shot in Hollywood in the spring of 1919. Again he helped out with the script. In the film he was strapped in a strait-jacket and suspended head downwards from a roof-top. After releasing himself he dropped on to an awning, then to the sidewalk and escaped. He also escaped from a deep well and a rope-sling bear trap. The second film, *Terror Island*, was shot in the autumn on Catalina Island. In this he escaped from a flooded submarine, rescued the heroine from a locked safe, and foiled again and again every effort by cannibals to eat him.

The films did well enough at the box-office, but it cannot be said that Houdini made any great mark in the history of the movies. He was handicapped by his total lack of acting ability. He was bashful in the scenes with the heroine and kissed her awkwardly. Romantic scenes were short enough in action films, but they were even briefer when Houdini was the lover. Directors could not persuade him to display a modicum of passion; he was too embarrassed.

Movies were now his major interest; they offered the alternative career he was seeking. He had no intention of confining himself to acting; he wanted to produce his own films. He realised the tremendous potential of the industry. Vaudeville bills were already including short films—cartoons, comedy, news— and he believed that one day movies would entirely replace vaudeville. Tastes in entertainment had changed, reflecting the postwar mood of restlessness. Life was faster. No audience would sit enthralled for an hour while he escaped hidden from their sight, as they had done ten years ago. So he decided to move with the times. As his first investment he bought a film developing corporation, and persuaded Dash to leave show business to manage it. This investment and his future plans needed money. His only way of raising this was to go back to vaudeville.

And all this time he was attending seances, but his mother had still not come back to him, at least not in any way he could believe. Mediums had given him messages from her, but these had always been vague. He had heard nothing evidential, nothing concrete. He wanted an intimate message, one that he alone could understand and know for certain that it came from her. It need not be a message, a word would do, especially if the word was FORGIVE, the one word he most wanted to hear. It seemed to him that he was asking the spiritualists for very little proof. Just give him that one word and he would believe that the dead could talk to the living.

The question of spirit communication obsessed him. He had begun to make pacts with each of his friends that whoever died first would try to communicate with the other. He invented secret codes and hand-grips that the medium must reproduce to prove the communication genuine. With all these people there were ties of affection, for he reasoned that those who loved him were the most likely to return. All these pacts were bound by love, and so the one he held in the greatest solemnity was the one he made with Bess.

Bess and he vowed that whoever died first would send a message consisting of ten words. The first word was ROSABELLE, the name that had such a special meaning for both of them. The remaining nine words would be in code, the same code they had used in their mind-reading act. These words were ANSWER TELL PRAY ANSWER LOOK TELL ANSWER ANSWER TELL. The code was based on ten key words or phrases, each of which stood for a number, which in turn represented the position of a letter in the alphabet.

PRAY	= 1	ANSWER	= B
ANSWER	= 2	TELL	= E
SAY	= 3	PRAY ANSWER	= L
NOW	= 4	LOOK	= I
TELL	= 5	TELL	= E
PLEASE	= 6	ANSWER ANSWER	= V
SPEAK	= 7	TELL	= E
QUICKLY	= 8		
LOOK	= 9		
BE QUICK	= 10		

So the nine letters of the code stood for the word BELIEVE. The full message was ROSABELLE BELIEVE.

Bess and he swore that neither of them would accept that any spirit message from the other was genuine unless it came in the exact formation of this code. Houdini expected that he would die first and he was determined to come back if this was at all possible. He would will it with all the force of his personality. He would come back to Bess through this code and prove that the dead could talk to the living. If it were true, he would demonstrate spirit communication so positively that no one on earth would ever be able to doubt again.

Chapter Seven

THE SILENT SPIRITS

In December 1919 he sailed in the *Mauretania* for a tour of Britain. This was his first visit in more than five years. He found the country in tune with his morbidity. The War had robbed countless people of their loved ones; far more than in America. Scarcely a family had not lost a father, a brother, or a son. In the streets mourning clothes predominated. Wherever he walked he saw in the faces of strangers his own pre-occupation with death. His act comprised the Needles Trick, Metamorphosis, and the Torture Cell. He also did challenge escapes, usually from wooden packing cases. He showed escape sequences from his films, and told his audiences that this was the last time they would see him in person, since he intended to devote himself to making movies.

His serial, *The Master Mystery,* was currently playing in British cinemas and this was creating a new demand for his act among the generation growing up, who had never seen him. No clothes line was safe from boys, who all wanted to imitate him by having themselves tied up. Crowds of barefooted urchins waited for him outside the stage door and ran beside him, cheering, as he walked to his hotel. Their poverty distressed him, and in some towns he bought hundreds of pairs of shoes to be distributed among poor children.

The British public were glad to see him again and the warmth of their welcome brought some relief to his spirit; but the only true repose he could find was in the graveyard. In February 1920, when he was playing at the Empire Theatre, Edinburgh, he went with Bess to visit the grave of the Great Lafayette, an old friend, who had once been the highest paid illusionist in vaudeville.

Nine years previously, when Lafayette had been performing at the Empire Theatre, a fire broke out backstage. The safety curtain was lowered, but the stage became an inferno. After the fire had been extinguished eleven bodies were found, all burnt beyond recognition. The body of Lafayette was identified by the charred costume, and then taken away to be prepared for burial. But later another body was found wearing the same costume. This was positively identified as Lafayette. The other corpse was that of his stage double. The grisly confusion fascinated Houdini. He envied Lafayette, the magician who had fooled people in death as well as in life.

Bess and he had brought some flowers as a tribute and two vases in which to arrange them. He set the flowers in their vases on the grave and asked Lafayette to give him a sign that he was present. The vases overturned. Bess wondered if her skirt had caught them. He set them upright and again they overturned. He thought this strange, but attributed it to sudden gusts of wind.

In Britain the heavy death toll of the War had led to a great resurgence of interest in spiritualism. There was an almost universal desire to speak with the dead and spiritualism flourished as never before. It had become an important force. Famous personalities from all walks of life embraced it. They spoke out and wrote in its support. Of these the man who made the greatest impact on the public was Sir Arthur Conan Doyle, and he was the man Houdini most wanted to meet.

Doyle was one of the best-known authors of the day, creator of Sherlock Holmes, writer of first-rate historical and adventure stories. Big and burly, he was regarded as a John Bull character with no nonsense about him. He was the epitome of the British belief in fair play. Through his own efforts he had righted two scandalous miscarriages of justice. He was a patriot and a sportsman, the two attributes most admired by his fellow countrymen. In his day he had been an amateur heavy-weight boxing champion and first-class cricketer. He had once taken the wicket of the great W. G. Grace. He could make a three figure break at billiards. Such a man was not readily associated with the shadows of the seance room.

Some said that his conversion to spiritualism was the result of an emotional breakdown caused by the loss of his son and brother in the War, but this was not so since he had publicly declared his faith two years before these events. His conversion, in 1916, had come as a blinding light. He believed that in spiritualism God had sent a new message of joy down to earth. He also believed that those to whom the message had been revealed had a sacred duty to pass it on at whatever cost of time, money, or labour. At the time of his conversion he was fifty-seven years old and he saw his life as having been a preparation for this great moment. For the past thirty years he had been fashioned by God into an instrument of His will. His books and reputation, all that had given him a name with the people now gave him a voice to which they would listen.

So he had gone forth, as the apostles had gone forth, to preach the good news. He had given up his lucrative writing and put his pen at the disposal of the movement. He wrote books, pamphlets, and newspaper articles. He lectured all over Britain to crowded audiences. His towering presence and burning sincerity made many converts. No one did more to publicise the movement. Whatever he said or wrote caused great controversy, making spiritualism front page news. He was often angered by the press who tended to play up the fraudulent side. All such attacks were regarded by him as persecutions, similar to those endured by the early Christians.

He was fanatical in his belief. He did not bring to the subject the logical, analytical brain of his greatest creation, Sherlock Holmes. To him reason had nothing to do with it; spiritualism was a revealed truth. He had no time for scientific investigators who demanded tests of the medium. In his opinion these investigators were handicapped by their own intellects, unable to perceive that the simple and obvious explanation was also the true one. He asked them this question. If in the greatest of all seances, that of the upper room on the day of Pentecost, a sceptic had insisted on test conditions of his own devising, where would the rushing winds and tongues of fire have been?

No, for him there was no doubt; he *knew* spiritualism was

true. Had he not seen his mother and his son, his brother and his nephew, as plainly as he ever saw them in life? His son had spoken of things unknown to the medium, who was bound and breathing deeply in his chair. He had seen materialised spirits walk round the room and join in the talk of the company. He had clasped their hands and inhaled the peculiar ozone-like smell of ectoplasm. He had seen heavy articles swimming in the air, untouched by human hands. He had seen objects from a distance projected into a room with closed doors and windows. He had seen faces of the dead glimmer up on a photographic plate which no hand but his had touched. He had listened to prophecies which were quickly fulfilled. He had received through the hands of his own wife notebooks of information which was utterly beyond her knowledge. No, if he could witness this and yet remain unconvinced that the dead were all around him, then he would have good cause to doubt his own sanity.

No wonder Houdini was anxious to meet Doyle. The man who had been given such conclusive proof was the very one to help him in his quest. He wrote to him and Doyle replied. They met and took an instant liking to each other. They were to become great friends. At first sight they seem an incongruous pair, as can be seen in photographs of them together; the tall patrician Englishman and the stocky, self-made Jew. But they had much in common. Both were profoundly honest men, serious and sincere, hard-working and dedicated. Both shared an obsession with death. Both were happily married. Houdini met Lady Doyle and their three children, all of whom believed implicitly in spiritualism. Doyle told him that Lady Doyle herself was a very fine medium. Death held no terrors for the children. They enjoyed talking to their dead relatives in the domestic seances organized by their parents.

During Houdini's tour of Britain, Doyle and he corresponded frequently. At the outset Houdini thought it best to define clearly where he stood on the subject of spiritualism. He told Doyle that although he was still a sceptic he was a seeker after truth. He was willing to be converted if he could find one genuine medium. He had tried hard to find such a medium, but so far he had failed. He wanted to believe because he longed so terribly to talk to his mother; but he had been given no proof, no evidence, and so the matter remained in question.

Doyle told him that proof would come in abundance, pressed down and overflowing; of that there was no doubt. Houdini wished that he could be as certain. But what about fraud, he asked, was there no possibility of fraud? Yes, Doyle admitted, there was fraud but far less than was commonly supposed. He explained that in the seance room most fraud was of two types, conscious and unconscious. Conscious fraud usually arose from a temporary failure of real psychic power and a subsequent attempt by the medium to replace it by imitation. And who could blame the medium? Psychic force came and went of its own accord. No one could turn it on and off like a tap. Unconscious fraud came when a medium was in a trance. In this state he was completely at the mercy of the spirits, some of whom were mischievous, even downright wicked, discrediting the medium by making him appear to cheat.

Houdini was not happy with this answer. He asked Doyle about *real* fraud, premeditated and deliberate. Doyle assured him that such fraud was very rare indeed, for what man could be so base as to mock the spirits of the dead? Such a man would be guilty of the most odious and blasphemous crime which a human being could commit. Again Houdini was not happy with the answer. He was beginning to realise that Doyle, while logical and rational in other matters, was so innocent and incorruptible over spiritualism that he could not conceive of any of his fellow spiritualists being otherwise. It followed that he could easily be duped by fake mediums. Houdini recalled his first visit to Doyle's home, when he had done some simple tricks to amuse the children. None of the children had been so mystified as Doyle himself. For the life of him he could not see how Houdini could possibly have done them. What chance had such a man against spook crooks steeped in trickery?

Houdini continued to press the question of fraud. Doyle told him that he was too interested in the negative side of spiritualism and that the time had come to seek out the positive. To aid him in this he gave him a list of mediums whom he knew to be honest. But he warned Houdini that he must approach the seances not in the spirit of a detective trailing a suspect but in that of a humble soul yearning for help. This need not preclude common sense in judging the results. A receptive state of mind was needed in order to produce the harmony which would encourage the spirits to come. Antagonism and scepticism were bound to drive them away. That was why most investigators ruined their chances before they began. Everything depended upon harmony; to disregard this was folly.

Through Doyle Houdini now had introductions to the best mediums in the land. He was determined to make full use of this unique opportunity, for if none of these could bring his mother back to him, then who could? He promised Doyle that he would attend the seances humbly and reverently, that he would put no obstruction in the medium's way, but would do all in his power to obtain results. After all, no one wanted to believe more than he did.

So his quest continued. He began sitting with the mediums recommended by Doyle. He was usually accompanied by Bess and her young niece, Julie Sawyer, who acted as his secretary and Bess's companion. Julie combined an innocent face with an alert, intelligent mind, and she was rapidly becoming an expert in detecting fraud. After each seance they compared notes. Houdini was not convinced by any of the mediums he visited. In his diary he expressed his disgust and rage at the ridiculous things they said and did; but his reports on them to Doyle were judicious and guarded. In no way was he playing a double game. So long as any hope of communication with his mother existed, he dare not offend the most important man in the spiritualist movement.

Doyle was puzzled that after all these seances Houdini had still not had the proof he sought, especially as he himself was getting the most astonishing results from the same mediums. To him the proof was so obvious that he simply could not understand Houdini's continuing scepticism. Some of the mediums told Doyle that Houdini's attitude was hostile. Houdini denied this and Doyle believed him. Why then, he wondered, had the truth of spiritualism not been revealed to him?

He continued to recommend mediums and Houdini visited all of them. During his six month stay in Britain he attended one hundred seances. The mediums passed on the usual vague messages from his mother, some even speaking in her voice. But not one of them came near to giving him the message he sought, or indeed any message that he could regard as evidential. He was enraged by the effrontery of these charlatans, especially those who impersonated his mother, but he still dared not protest openly. He continued to live in hope that some sign would be given. He wanted so much to believe that he was reluctant to say that all of it was humbug.

As Houdini toured the country Doyle followed his exploits in the newspapers, reading again and again of his baffling escapes from the Torture Cell and packing cases. Houdini had assured him that all these escapes were made by natural means, but Doyle was beginning to have his doubts. These doubts were shared by other British spiritualists, among them James Hewat Mackenzie, president of the Psychic College. During a performance at the Grand Theatre, Islington, Mackenzie had been a member of the committee on stage when Houdini escaped from the Torture Cell. While Houdini was escaping in the secrecy of his cabinet, Mackenzie had experienced a great loss of physical energy, such as was felt by sitters in materialising seances. He had no doubt that inside the Cell Houdini was dematerialising himself. Doyle was inclined to agree with this conclusion. He found it most suggestive that Houdini insisted on having a committee on stage during his escape. They, poor dupes, thought they were there to detect trickery, while in reality Houdini depended on them for the stock of vital energy he needed in order to dematerialise himself. No wonder such a man came up against a blank wall in the seance room.

He wrote to Houdini asking why he was seeking a demonstration of the supernatural when he was giving one himself all the time. He begged him to consider that perhaps the reason why proof of spirit communication was cut off from him was that he was not playing the game with his marvellous power. Such a gift was not given to one man in a hundred million and it was not given to be trivialised and commercialised. Houdini should not be amusing and misleading the public, asking them to regard a startling manifestation of miraculous power as no more than a very clever trick.

Doyle, unawares, had touched on the great question that had troubled Houdini throughout his professional life. Could technique, when carried to its furthest point, unleash some psychic force to give a result which could truly be called miraculous? He had never found the answer, and so he told Doyle that so far as he was aware all his escapes were accomplished by natural means, and that if he did possess some wondrous power than he did not know it.

Doyle saw nothing irreconcilable in this and his own conclusion. So little was known about these great mysteries. It could be possible for a man to be a powerful medium all his life, to use that power continually, and yet never realise that the gift was supernatural. It could be that inside the packing case, or the Torture Cell, Houdini was in a semi-trance, making confused efforts to escape, and then finding himself outside, not fully grasping how he came to be there. From his own knowledge of Houdini he knew that the man did not fully understand himself or his motives. He was not a clear thinker, but emotional and intuitive. He had no philosophy by which he could explain his life. Doyle in his time had met many men in many places, but he considered Houdini far and away the most intriguing person he had ever encountered. He was planning to visit America on a lecture tour. There he hoped to meet Houdini again and solve this enigma.

*

On 3 July Houdini had sailed for home. On arriving in New York he went straight to his mother's grave. For the rest of his life this was to be his first act on returning to the city and his last one on leaving. While in New York he visited the grave every day, sometimes at dawn or at fifteen minutes after midnight, the instant of her death. He would tell her how much he missed her and how much he loved her. He would tell her that he was sparing no efforts to contact her. Before leaving he would embrace and kiss the earth that contained her.

Thoughts of death were with him all the time. In September, when John Sargent, his private secretary, lay dying, he hurried to his side. Sargent was one of the friends with whom he had made a pact that whoever died first would try to communicate with the other. Now Sargent lay on his death bed. He clasped Houdini's hand and renewed the vow he had made, repeating the key word he would give if ever he could make contact. He swore that he would come back if he could; he swore this with all his remaining strength. The next day he died. In the months that followed, Houdini attended seance after seance, in the belief that if any man could come back to him that man would be Sargent. They had been so close that he was certain he would have received the sign had his friend wanted to call him. But the sign had not been given, although the supposed spirit of Sargent had come through several times. Why, Houdini wondered, had this not happened? No one could accuse him of being unwilling to receive such a sign. He could not accept Doyle's theory that the spirit world was closed to him. Why should it be? He believed in life after death. He was seeking with all his heart and mind for enlightenment. Why then, if spiritualism were true, should this be denied him?

It seemed more and more likely that he would receive no answer this side of the grave, and in the meantime he had his living to make. The movie industry was booming and he was determined to become one of its leaders. He already owned a film developing business, managed by his brother Dash, and at the beginning of 1921 he went into the production side. He formed the Houdini Picture Corporation, with himself as president. His first production was *The Man from Beyond,* with himself as the star. He also wrote the script. Although he hired a director, Burton King, who had directed *The Master Mystery*, his control over the movie was total. The reels were to be processed and printed by the Houdini Film Development Corporation, and he himself would cut and edit them.

He had written a good script. Members of an arctic expedition discover a man frozen in a block of ice. They chop him free and find that a state of suspended animation has kept him alive. He had been frozen for one hundred years. They take him back to America, where he has to cope with the complexities of twentieth century life. He is also searching for his long-dead sweetheart and finds her reincarnation in one of her great-granddaughters.

In May the company travelled to Niagara Falls to film the rescue sequence, which was to form the climax of the film. In this Houdini was to rescue the heroine above the Falls, after her capsized canoe had plunged downwards. Both he and the heroine's double wore a safety device under their clothes, a harness with a steel-wire rope attached, operated by a drum on the shore. But the device did not work effectively and as a result the rescue was more hair-raising than even Houdini had intended. He and the girl were swept forward by the raging torrent, and he rescued her on the very brink of the Falls. This sensational sequence was praised by the critics when the movie was first shown in April 1922.

In that same month Sir Arthur Conan Doyle, together with his wife and family, arrived in New York, to begin a lecture tour on spiritualism. There were probably about a million people in America who called themselves spiritualists and Doyle hoped that there would be a great many more before he left. At Carnegie Hall he lectured to capacity audiences and went on to speak in other eastern cities, including Boston, Philadelphia, and Buffalo. As in Britain, his lectures inaugurated a great public controversy over spiritualism. In May Doyle and his wife visited the Houdinis in their home. Houdini was delighted to entertain such a distinguished man in his house, not least because of the opportunity this gave him of showing off his collection. Doyle had no idea what was in store for him. The result of Houdini's mania for collecting was about to be revealed in all its enormity.

There were thousands upon thousands of books on magic, spiritualism, and all aspects of the occult. Not only books but periodicals, newspaper cuttings, pamphlets, and letters. These filled scores of packing cases stacked away in the cellars. The rooms above contained mountains of unshelved books, trunks crammed with documents, and crated stage illusions used by famous magicians. The floors were littered with hundreds of locks, manacles, and chains. The place was more like a warehouse than a home. Some rooms were so full that it was impossible to move about in them. Throughout Europe and America he had strode into book shops and bought up the entire stock, sometimes twenty thousand volumes at a time. His collection contained at least eight private libraries, and crates of fresh additions were arriving every week. The bulk of his vast income was spent on his collection, which was by no means confined to magic and the occult. There was a drama section with an estimated two hundred thousand theatre programmes and two hundred and fifty thousand autographed papers, all disorganised and uncatalogued. The sheer mass of it was daunting, sickening. There were letters written by Edmund Kean, Jenny Lind, and Mrs Siddons. There was the private diary of David Garrick. As Doyle picked his way from room to room, it was as though he was walking through the interstices of Houdini's chaotic brain. There were the autographs of all but two of the signers of the Declaration of Independence, Martin Luther's Bible, Edgar Allan Poe's writing desk, one of the earliest electric chairs to be used in America, and a heel from the last shoes worn by Robert Heller, the magician, with a signed authentication from the undertaker, who had removed the heels because the magician was too tall to fit into the coffin. Doyle left the house, stunned. It had been a strange experience, appalling yet wonderful.

*

During June Doyle and his family were resting at Atlantic City, the popular seaside resort on the Jersey Shore. Houdini and Bess joined them for a weekend. Doyle was glad of the opportunity to have a quiet word with Houdini. He had been hearing from American spiritualists of his connexion with Joe Rinn and other psychic investigators who were considered to be opposed to the movement. He told him that he had the reputation of being a bitterly prejudiced enemy who was out to make trouble, but he himself did not believe this. He went on to speak of the marvellous phenomena he had witnessed in America, but it seemed to Houdini that all these manifestations had been no more than spook tricks.

They talked of spirit photography. Doyle showed him a photograph of a coffin covered with flowers. The face of the dead woman was visible above the coffin. There were two other spirit faces, a man and a woman, on either side of the coffin. Houdini thought the photograph an obvious fake, but he did not say this outright as he knew that it would hurt Doyle. So he merely hinted at the possibility of fraud. Even this shocked Doyle. He said that there was no man so vile and despicable that he would commit fraud in so hallowed a place as a graveyard. Houdini never ceased to be amazed at Doyle's innocence; never in his life had he encountered anyone so trusting.

The following afternoon, 17 June, Houdini and Bess were sitting in deck-chairs on the beach, sunning themselves. Behind them were the ornate hotels and crowded boardwalk. Before them the great Atlantic waves thundered and foamed over the sandy beach. It was a glorious day and the sea was filled with bathers. Handsome bronzed lifeguards stood ready for action, surrounded by admiring girls.

Then Houdini became aware that Doyle was approaching. He could see his towering figure picking its way through the crowds. Doyle was excited. He told Houdini that Lady Doyle wanted to give him an automatic writing seance straight away. He apologised to Bess, but the seance was for Houdini alone. Lady Doyle preferred it that way.

Houdini followed him back to the Ambassador Hotel, where they were all staying. They went into the sitting room of Doyle's suite, where Lady Doyle awaited them. The curtains were drawn against the afternoon sun. The three of them sat at a table, on which lay a writing pad and two pencils. Doyle bowed his head and said a short prayer, beseeching God to let them have a sign from their friends in the world beyond the grave. Houdini closed his eyes and prayed, trying to help the seance as much as he could. All was quiet in the room and from outside came the muffled roar of the Atlantic rollers.

Lady Doyle took a pencil in her right hand, then rested the hand on the table. Doyle caressed it as though to aid her. The hand began to jerk spasmodically. She explained that a spirit had taken hold of her in a most energetic manner. She asked the spirit if it believed in God. Her hand hit the table three times, signifying yes. She drew the sign of the cross on the writing pad. Then she asked if the spirit was that of Houdini's mother. Again her hand struck the table three times. Houdini concentrated with all his mind, trying to imagine that his beloved mother was really in the room. He thought of trivial things they had often done together, hoping that if she were truly present she would refer to one of them. Lady Doyle began to write rapidly. She filled a page of the pad and Doyle tore it off and passed it across the table to Houdini. This is what he read : —

'Oh, my darling, thank God, thank God, at last I'm through —I've tried, oh so often—now I am happy. Why, of course, I want to talk to my boy—my own beloved boy. Friends, thank you with all my heart for this.'

Doyle tore off another sheet and passed it to Houdini.

'You have answered the cry of my heart—and of his—God bless him—a thousand-fold, for all his life for me—never had a mother such a son—tell him not to grieve, soon he'll get all the evidence he is anxious for. Yes, we know—tell him, I want him to write in his own home. It will be far better so.'

Lady Doyle scribbled on. Doyle tore sheet after sheet from the pad and tossed each across to Houdini, who, pale and grim, continued to read.

'I will work with him—he is so, so dear to me—I am preparing so sweet a home for him which one day in God's good time, he will come to—it is one of my great joys preparing it for the future—

'I am so happy in this life—it is so full and joyous—my only shadow has been that my beloved one hasn't known how often

I have been with him all the while—here away from my heart's darling—combining my work thus in this life of mine.'

Lady Doyle wrote feverishly. From time to time Doyle soothed her, as if admonishing the spirit not to be too forcible with her. The message poured on and on : —

'It is so different over here, so much larger and bigger and more beautiful—so lofty—all sweetness around one—nothing that hurts and we see our beloved ones on earth—that is such a joy and comfort to us—Tell him I love him more than ever— the years only increase it—and his goodness fills my soul with gladness and thankfulness. Oh, just this, it *is* me. I want him only to know that—that—I have bridged the gulf—That is what I wanted, oh so much—Now I can rest in peace—How soon—'

At this point Doyle stayed his wife's hand and asked Houdini if he would like to ask his mother a question. Her answer would prove to him that she was in the room. He spoke as if Houdini's mother was in reality standing by her son's side. Houdini was so anguished that he could not bring himself to reply. Doyle suggested the question, 'Can my mother read my mind?' Houdini nodded his assent and Lady Doyle started to write : —

'I *always* read my beloved son's mind—his dear mind—there is so much I want to say to him—but—I am almost overwhelmed by this joy of talking to him once more—it is almost too much to get through—the joy of it—thank you, thank you, thank you, friend, with all my heart for what you have done for me this day —God bless you, too, Sir Arthur, for what you are doing for us —for us over here—who so need to get in touch with our beloved ones on the earth plane—'

As Doyle passed each page across the table, he observed that Houdini was under some great emotional strain. The message went on : —

'If only the world knew this great truth—how different life would be for men and women—Go on, let nothing stop you— great will be your reward hereafter—Goodbye—I brought you, Sir Arthur, and my darling son together—I felt you were the one man who might help us to pierce the veil—and I was right— Bless him, bless him, bless him, I say from the depths of my soul—he fills my heart and later we shall be together—oh, so happy—a happiness awaits him that he has never dreamed of—tell him I am with him—just tell him that I'll soon make him know how close I am all the while—his eyes will soon be opened —Goodbye again—God's blessing be on you all—'

The message ended. Lady Doyle leaned back in her chair. Houdini sat silent with bowed head. Doyle and Lady Doyle looked at each other triumphantly. Then Houdini picked up the pencil Lady Doyle had been using and wrote one word on the pad. When he looked up, Doyle was amazed to see in his eyes that unfocused look which comes to a medium in a trance. He believed that in that instant he had surprised the master secret of Houdini. He picked up the pad and read the word Houdini had written. It was as though an electric shock had gone through him. Houdini had written the name, 'Powell'. Ellis Powell, a spiritualist friend of Doyle, had died a few days previously. Doyle was now totally convinced that Houdini was a medium, for he had written the name of the one person most likely to try to come back to him. He told Houdini this, but Houdini would not agree. He said that he had been thinking of Frederick Eugene Powell, the magician, who at the time was having difficulties with his act. Doyle would not have this at all, but Houdini did not stay to argue the matter.

He left the darkened room and went out into the bright sunlight, searching for Bess among the crowds of holidaymakers. His mind was in a turmoil of anger, bitterness, and despair. He clutched in his hand the message that was supposed to have come from his beloved mother—a vague message containing nothing evidential, signed with a cross when she had been a practising Jew, and written in fluent English, a language she could barely speak let alone write. That was why he had been so grim-faced and silent during the seance; he had been hiding from the Doyles his intense disappointment. Surely if his mother was to come she would have come on this most holy occasion when her son, together with two good and gentle people, had been praying for her to come. But she had not come. What was there left for him to believe in after this?

E

Chapter Eight

A FORBIDDEN PATH

A week after the Atlantic City seance Doyle and his family returned to England. The controversy he had inaugurated in America was still raging. Houdini made his presence felt in the argument by writing letters to newspapers. His pre-occupation with the subject spilled over into his professional life. He was travelling the country making personal appearances at showings of *The Man from Beyond*. His promotion talk was less about the film than about spiritualism. He was still trying to keep an open mind on the subject, but he found this difficult since his seance with the Doyles, and his talk was deeply sceptical. He told his audiences that no one had tried harder than he to discover the truth of the matter, but in all his investigations he had never come across one genuine medium. He told them of the many dishonest mediums he had encountered, and he duplicated some of their tricks.

By the autumn the study and exposure of mediums had become his overriding interest. He lectured to civic organisations, telling his audiences that no one knew more about the subject than he. Characteristically he issued a challenge to all mediums that he would give five thousand dollars if he could not duplicate any of their phenomena. This did not impress the spiritualists, who argued that duplication did not invalidate phenomena, that to materialise a human form on stage with the aid of elaborate machinery could not be compared to an ectoplasmic manifestation of a spirit in the simple setting of a private house.

The spiritualists were also saying that Houdini in his heart knew that spiritualism was true, but would not admit it. Before leaving America Doyle had told his friends about the Atlantic City seance. Houdini had left the seance without discussing it with Doyle. He had not dared because of the strength of his feelings. Hence Doyle and his wife believed that they had convinced him of the truth of spiritualism. So they told their friends how Houdini had been stunned into silence by the message from his mother, and that soon he would announce his change of heart.

But far from announcing any conversion Houdini continued to publicise his doubts. On 30 October, in the New York *Sun*, he stated that he was perfectly willing to believe, but he had never seen or heard anything that could convince him that there was a possibility of communication with the dead. Doyle read this and wrote to Houdini saying that the statement could not be reconciled with what Doyle had seen with his own eyes. He had seen what his wife, the purest of mediums, had given Houdini, and he had seen the effect this had had upon him. Houdini had also written down the name of Ellis Powell, the one man who might be expected to communicate with Doyle. In Doyle's view Houdini had been given his proof. The responsibility of accepting or rejecting it rested with him, and it was a very real and lasting responsibility.

Doyle's letter placed Houdini in a dilemma. He did not want to reveal that the message from his mother had been written in a language she barely understood; he had no wish to hurt or discredit the Doyles. But he could not allow the spiritualists a false victory. He decided that his best move would be to make a sworn statement about the Atlantic City seance. On 19 December he appeared before the Notary Public for the Bronx district of New York City and swore that he could not accept that the letter written by Lady Doyle had come from his mother or that the spirit of Doyle's friend, Ellis Powell, had guided his hand. He put this on record so that after his death the truth would be known.

Spiritualism was headline news. Mediums multiplied all over the country to cope with the growing number of converts. There was money to be made and the movement was exploited for all it was worth. Even respectable business enterprises were quick to take advantage of it. The management of *Scientific American* decided that a good way to boost the circulation of their periodical would be to investigate evidence of psychic phenomena. They offered two prizes of two thousand five hundred dollars each, one for a physical manifestation of a psychic nature produced under scientific control, and the other for an authentic spirit photograph made under strict test conditions.

A committee was appointed to judge the applicants. Its distinguished members included Dr William McDougall, Professor of Psychology, Harvard University; Dr Daniel Fisk Comstock, late of the Massachusetts Institute of Technology; Dr Walter Franklin Prince, Research Officer of the American Society of Psychical Research; and Hereward Carrington, psychic investigator and well-known writer on the subject. One more place on the committee remained to be filled and that was reserved for a magician, for it had been noted that in Europe mediums were reluctant to sit with any committee that included a magician. It was becoming recognised that while scientists were needed to evaluate genuine phenomena, if such existed, they were no better qualified to check up on fraud than the man in the street. They were deceived just as readily by magicians on the stage as anyone else in the audience, and so it was equally easy for them to be deceived by the tricks of mediums.

When the *Scientific American* committee was being formed, the choice of magician lay between Houdini and Thurston. Houdini was finally chosen as being the more competent of the two. He had already shown an interest in psychic investigation and no living magician had so profound a knowledge of trickery. Houdini received the invitation to serve on the committee as no more than his due. He would have been astounded had he not been chosen. In no way did he feel inferior to his distinguished fellow members. Quite the reverse. In his view he was an expert not only on fraud but also on all aspects of spiritualism, and as such he regarded himself as the most informed and authoritative member of the committee.

At the end of 1922, when the committee was formed, Houdini's financial affairs were in a mess. *Haldane of the Secret*

Service, the second full-length feature film to be produced by his company, had been released and had proved to be a flop. He was again the star, this time playing a government agent investigating a gang of counterfeiters. He promoted the film extensively, but to no avail. The receipts did not meet the production costs. There was no reserve finance and so his career as a film producer was at an end. He had no alternative but to return to vaudeville. Dash continued to manage the Houdini Film Development Corporation for a while, but this was making little profit and eventually he too returned to vaudeville.

So at the very time Houdini was invited to join the *Scientific American* committee he had signed a contract that was to take him on a six month tour of the West. But he was determined to serve on the committee and he promised to cancel bookings whenever he was called for an investigation. The Torture Cell was the main feature of his act and the Upside-Down Strait-Jacket Escape his main outdoor stunt, but he continued to do bridge jumps and underwater escapes from packing cases. The way these stunts were staged made them more dangerous than ever. In their intensity they were sometimes unbearable to watch and people turned their eyes away, fearing not so much for his physical safety as for the destiny of his immortal soul, for they sensed that he was embarking on a forbidden path. Doyle read of these stunts and begged him to stop.

But Houdini could not stop. He was taking himself to the threshold of death in the hope of going out of his body, if only for a moment and transcending into another sphere, where he would be surrounded by the spirits of the dead. Perhaps in that place, in that instant, his mother would come to him. How else could he speak to her? Try as he may to keep it alive his hope of spirit communication was dying. What then remained? Should he kill himself and go to his mother with a great sin upon his soul? He hesitated to do that. What then remained? Only the loss of his sanity and the companionship of the mad.

His visits to lunatic asylums became more frequent. He began to compile notes on inmates driven mad by spiritualism. He was also compiling a file on suicide cases in which spiritualism had played a part. He found these cases fell into two categories: those who had killed themselves in despair and those who had killed themselves, and even other members of their family including children, the quicker to join some loved one beyond the grave. Spiritualism claimed to bring consolation. It had brought none to these people and it had brought none to him. It had brought him only great anguish and constant fear for his reason and the sanctity of his life.

*

In April 1923 Doyle began a second lecture tour in America. On his previous visit he had confined himself to the Eastern states; this time he intended visiting the West. As before, he opened his campaign in New York, speaking at Carnegie Hall to audiences which were, in the main, sympathetic. Joe Rinn had been asked to attend on behalf of the New York *American* and he used the occasion to launch a devastating attack on Doyle. He said that Doyle, like all spiritualists, accepted the basic rule that anything antagonistic prevented a medium from producing phenomena; a rule that had favoured every spook crook since the Fox sisters started the racket. Hence Doyle rejected all scientific investigations that controlled the medium. Hence he could state that no medium he had endorsed had been shown to be fraudulent in the sense that would be accepted by a spiritualist. Doyle, invincible in his faith, was unable to see himself for what he was, a deluded fool.

In attacking Doyle publicly Rinn had done what Houdini could not bring himself to do, but many spiritualists, aware of his close association with Rinn, were already convinced that he shared this attitude. True, he had not spoken out personally against Doyle, but no one could attack spiritualism without attacking Doyle; the two were inseparable. Doyle's spiritualist friends warned him against Houdini, but Doyle told them that they had got it all wrong. Houdini was fighting a last ditch battle, wrestling with his conscience, before accepting the evidence of the Atlantic City seance and publicly announcing his conversion to spiritualism. And what a catch that would be for the movement!

So Doyle advised his friends to be patient and wait for the ripe and juicy apple to fall.

In May the two men met in Denver. Doyle was lecturing there and Houdini was performing in vaudeville. Doyle saw his act and afterwards went to his dressing room for a talk. They were soon arguing over trickery in spirit photography. Doyle said that he was as capable as Houdini of detecting fraud. Houdini said that he did not think so. Doyle told him that if he wanted proof of spirit photography he should visit Alexander Martin, the Denver photographer, whose pictures of the living also showed faces of the dead. Houdini and his assistant, James Collins, called on Martin. They found him an elderly unassuming man, living in poor circumstances. He took a photograph of them. When the plate was developed the print showed four spirit faces in the background. Houdini had his photograph taken alone and five spirit faces appeared on the print. Houdini was convinced that a double-exposure technique had been used. The heads of the so-called spirits had been cut from other photographs and exposed on a plate, the centre area of which was masked. This plate was then used in photographing the sitter. When developed the faces appeared on the print and seemed to be surrounding him. Again he was amazed that Doyle with his brilliant mind could be so easily fooled.

As yet both had been able to avoid a public argument, but Doyle's tour was being given massive coverage in the press and reporters were constantly badgering each of them for quotes about the other. In Denver, Doyle gave an interview to a reporter from the Denver *Express,* who asked for an opinion about Houdini's five thousand dollar challenge that he could duplicate any psychic phenomena produced by mediums. Doyle said that his mother had been brought back by mediums and to convince him Houdini would have to bring her back as clearly as they had done. In the *Express,* under huge headlines it was reported that Doyle had offered to bring back the spirit of his mother in order to confute Houdini, and that he backed his belief with five thousand dollars and challenged Houdini to do the same. When Doyle read this he was angry and dismayed. He assured Houdini that he had never issued such a challenge. Houdini laughed and told him that being misquoted in the American press was one of those trials every public figure had to endure.

The press were also anxious to know Doyle's opinion of the *Scientific American* awards. Doyle said that the enterprise was a farce, that no medium could be expected to produce phenomena under the clinical conditions imposed by the committee. It was his conviction that no medium of repute would participate. In this he had so far been proved correct. The quality of the applicants was certainly low, but there were two among them who could be regarded as serious contenders.

The first of these was George Valiantine. He gave two seances for the committee while Houdini was on tour. All in all he was an impressive performer. A trumpet not only floated about the room but also tapped the committee members on their heads. Houdini came to New York for the third seance. The committee had taken some precautions against fraud. Unknown to the medium his chair had been wired, so that should he ever leave his seat under the cover of the darkness prevailing during the seance, a light would flash in the control room and the time would be noted. After the seance, when these times were compared, the committee were able to establish that whenever phenomena had occurred in the seance room Valiantine was not in his chair. Houdini denounced him as a fraud and immediately released the story of the exposure to the press. The rest of the committee were dismayed at this, for the news should have been first announced in the *Scientific American*. Moreover, although the wiring device had been decided on while Houdini was still on the road, the story read as though he had been the one who had exposed the medium. It seemed to them that he was taking over the committee, as though fearing that without his presence they would endorse someone who was a fraud. They were offended by his attitude, because he so obviously believed that they could be fooled while he could not.

Unfortunately they were to make fools of themselves over the next contender of any merit. Nino Pecoraro was a twenty-four year old medium from Naples. During the seance bells rang and tambourines jingled. Houdini was playing Little Rock, Arkansas, at the time. The committee wired him to come at once to witness the medium who could produce phenomena even though roped hand and foot to his chair. Houdini arrived just as the next seance with Pecoraro was about to begin. To his utter amazement he found the committee preparing to bind the medium with one long length of rope. He told them that this was the easiest way to gain slack. He cut the rope into short pieces and bound the medium personally. The seance began, but although the committee sat for one and a half hours there were no manifestations. Again it seemed to the public that the committee would have awarded the prize to a fraud had it not been for Houdini, and again it seemed to the committee that he was just as interested in showing them up as in showing up fraudulent mediums.

Yet Houdini's high-handed behaviour is easily explained. He had begun to realise that by becoming a member of the committee he had placed himself in a vulnerable position. He was lecturing on every possible occasion at universities, colleges, and civic organisations. Although he was always careful to state that he was not attacking spiritualism itself but only the rogues that flourished within its ranks, the burden of his argument was overwhelmingly against the movement. He lived in daily dread that his fellow members of the committee like other academics before them—Sir William Crookes, Cesare Lombroso, Sir Oliver Lodge—would endorse a fraudulent medium. Then his would be the only dissenting voice and who would listen to it? Their words would carry more weight than his, and the reputation he was winning as an effective psychic investigator would be ruined. So every fraud must be exposed dramatically and publicly.

He had in effect launched a one-man campaign against spiritualism and his obsession with fraud led him to make indiscreet remarks about Doyle, which were widely reported in the press. He was reported as saying that Doyle was a sucker who had endorsed every spook crook in the business. When Doyle challenged him about this, Houdini said that he had been misquoted as Doyle had been in the Denver *Express*. He was reported as saying that Doyle had been gullible enough to endorse the notorious Masked Medium, the biggest crook of them all. Doyle had not even met the woman and he issued a denial to the press. This distressed him for he hated fighting with a friend in public, but he had to correct Houdini's statements or else they would be believed.

Doyle was making all allowances, but as he saw the situation it was no use Houdini claiming, as he always did, that he had been misquoted. He knew that Houdini was excitable, voluble, spoke without thinking. No doubt the reporters put words into his mouth. But he could not claim that all his words were misquoted; he must rest to some extent on what he said. He asked Houdini how long their friendship could survive such an ordeal. That friendship had been declining since the Atlantic City seance. Doyle had been patiently waiting for Houdini to acknowledge the truth of the message he had received through Lady Doyle. It had now become clear that he was not going to do so. This saddened Doyle. He was utterly convinced that the message was genuine and he regarded Houdini's scepticism as sheer perversity. He could only conclude that Houdini was not one hundred per cent intellectually honest; that he would never admit to one single instance of genuine mediumship, such as that of his wife, for if he did the case for spiritualism was proved, regardless of the hundreds of frauds he claimed to have encountered. Grant this one instance and his whole argument fell to the ground. Hence he would never grant that one case. Everything had to be fraud.

By the end of 1923 Doyle was expressing surprise that Houdini was still writing to him. He told him that he had no wish to offend him, but he must realise that he could not have it both ways. He could not bitterly and offensively attack a subject and expect courtesies from those who honoured it. He must be made aware that his statements were resented.

So Doyle and Houdini found themselves at war, campaigning against each other in the press and on the public platform. Intoxicated by his new-found role in life, Houdini was impervious to the pain he was causing Doyle. He resented the time he had to spend on the vaudeville stage; he wanted to be speaking to the whole wide world. His lectures were not reasoned arguments but diatribes. He felt too strongly about the subject. Lashing out in all directions he often spoiled his case. Doyle wondered how he reconciled his conflicting statements. Spiritualists could prove so many of these wrong as to throw doubts on those that were true. But who, they asked, could treat Houdini with anything but contempt? What was he but a renegade medium, who refused to acknowledge the true source of his power; a man of scepticism so profound that he would not have believed even had the risen Christ appeared before him; a madman raging mindlessly against the light.

Yet his state of mind was understandable. Before his mother's death he had regarded mediums as no more than confidence tricksters of a peculiarly nasty kind, but he had felt no personal involvement. Fools and their money would always be parted. This detachment had gone when mediums presumed to act as intermediaries between himself and his dead mother, passing on vague messages, speaking in her voice. He had been enraged by these charlatans, but dared not protest openly for fear of antagonising the spiritualist movement and cutting himself off from a genuine medium. His over-riding desire to talk to his mother had kept him going to seances, but with failure after failure that hope had died, and as it died his bitterness and sense of outrage had grown. Now he was compelled to defend not only his mother but all the dead against the blasphemy of the spiritualists. And the violence of his denunciation, had the spiritualists the ears to hear, reflected the intensity of his wish that their belief could be true.

*

The course of his life had completely changed. In February 1924 he signed with Coit-Albee Lyceum to give twenty-five lectures throughout America. The highest paid performer in vaudeville had elected to do one-night-stands for a lecturer's wage. But for Houdini the money was worth renouncing. He had found what he had been seeking all his life—a role to play in the great world, a deed to do for humanity. He was a public speaker, recognised as an authority on his subject, and sometimes lecturing in the same halls where Doyle had lectured. But he was aware that Doyle as a lecturer had an advantage. He was a distinguished and honoured personality; his words carried more weight than his own. Yet in one respect Houdini knew himself to be superior —he was an incomparable showman. He had observed that while Doyle's lectures had been invariably well-attended they had not always been the turn-aways they could have been. This was because they had not been properly publicised, at least not to his way of thinking. Moreover, while the lectures had been interesting they could hardly be called exciting.

So when Houdini went on tour as a lecturer he did not leave the showman behind. As always he did outdoor stunts and challenge escapes to bring in the crowds. The lectures themselves were an irresistible mixture of instruction and entertainment. He not only explained how the mediums produced their effects but actually did them himself. Tables levitated, musical instruments played, and messages appeared on blank slates, all apparently without human aid. The audiences loved it.

In England Doyle read of Houdini's lecture tour. He was dismayed at all the razzmatazz and ballyhoo concerning a belief he held in veneration. He thought such presentation was disgusting and degrading. He believed that Houdini was doing it just for the publicity, that his obsession with advertising himself had swallowed up his scruples. Houdini, for his part, still did not realise how deeply he was offending Doyle. He even wrote to him asking for some facts, which he wished to use in his lectures, Doyle refused to send them, saying that Houdini only wanted them so that he could twist them in some way against himself and his cause.

In April Houdini celebrated his fiftieth birthday. He could not believe that he had lived for half a century; he felt so young. In that same month he published his most substantial book. *A Magician Among the Spirits*. It created quite a stir and people remarked on how far removed he now was from the world of show business. The book was indeed a remarkable achievement. He depicted the development of spiritualism as a history of fraud. He did not mince his words. All mediums were termed human vultures. He argued that spiritualism brought more distress than comfort. He instanced the many cases of suicide and insanity. He enumerated the criminal uses to which spiritualism was put. He described how the big-time operators gathered information about their clients by employing spies strategically placed to listen in on conversations—elevator boys, switchboard girls, waiters in restaurants, chauffeurs, and domestic servants.

One medium employed a quiet couple to mingle with mourners at funerals. Another owned a beauty parlour where gossip was recorded. One operated a Turkish Bath where all clothes were searched and letters and notebooks read, while the patrons relaxed and perspired. Some bribed employees in the Bureau of Records, tapped telephones and intercepted mail. Others employed prostitutes. There were those whose so-called spirit-guides advised their clients on the purchase of stocks and shares, or suggested that an accomplice of the medium should handle all their financial affairs. The world of spiritualism, as depicted by Houdini, was a world of evil incarnate, where mediums hounded their victims to drink, drugs, madness, and shameful death. The book was described as a revelation, and a revelation it was; that of a man who turns over a stone to reveal the underside crawling with loathsome obscene creatures.

In another chapter he described his relationship with Doyle. He said that he admired Doyle and was proud of his friendship. He considered Doyle to be a brilliant man and a deep thinker, but also an unreasoning fanatic on the subject of spiritualism. It was impossible to convince him of fraud; he insisted mediums were genuine even after they themselves had confessed their deceit. Not caring now for Doyle's feelings, Houdini gave a full account of the Atlantic City seance and affirmed again that he did not accept the message as having come from his mother. He concluded by stating that in all the seances he had attended he had never seen anything to convince him that it was possible to communicate with the dead. Therefore Doyle and he could never agree.

Astonishingly he wrote to Doyle offering to send him a copy of the book. The letter remained unanswered.

Chapter Nine

THE ENCHANTRESS

Houdini's position now seemed unassailable as the man no medium could fool, the supreme mysteriarch, so deeply versed in trickery, that no human being could confront him with a mystery which he could not solve. Yet they still came forward, confident that they would be the one to outwit the great Houdini. There was, for example, Joaquin Maria Argamasilla, the man with the X-ray eyes. In May he arrived from Spain, claiming that with his supernormal vision he could see through gold, silver, copper, and other metals. He had baffled scientists in Spain and France, and now he prepared to baffle Houdini. An inscribed card was placed in a metal box and the lid was closed. He held the box in front of his eyes and read the inscription on the card. A watch was set to a certain time and the case of the watch was closed. He held the watch in his hand, focused his eyes on it and read the exact time.

Everyone murmured wonderingly, except Houdini. He had observed that the Spaniard moved the watch about in his hand while focusing it for his X-ray vision, and this gave him the opportunity to slip the case open and close it deftly. Houdini had come prepared. He gave Argamasilla a watch with a case that could not be readily opened, and this time the Spaniard's supernormal vision failed him. Then Houdini challenged Argamasilla to see through two metal boxes which he himself had designed. The Spaniard refused, saying that he could only work with his own boxes. Houdini had examined these and found the hasps and lids so constructed that Argamasilla could gain a quick glance inside without the spectators spotting the movement.

It seemed to Houdini that the exposure of Argamasilla would be the only victory of consequence he would gain that year. All was quiet on the spiritualist front. The *Scientific American* awards were still open, but they were not attracting any mediums worthy of his attention. Spiritualism was still news. Indeed a rival periodical, *Science and Invention*, was offering its own prize of one thousand dollars for proof of psychic phenomena. Joe Rinn had been invited to serve on their committee. He was pleased to accept. He had been somewhat piqued at being left off the *Scientific American* committee after all his years of experience as a psychic investigator. He celebrated his appointment by adding to the *Science and Invention* prize his own prize of ten thousand dollars.

There were now rich pickings for any genuine medium who cared to come forward. He or she could claim five thousand dollars from Houdini, two thousand five hundred dollars from *Scientific American*, one thousand dollars from *Science and Invention*, and ten thousand dollars from Joe Rinn. A total of eighteen thousand five hundred dollars. But even with this considerable sum at stake there were no takers of any merit. The sceptics claimed this as a victory, but the believers saw it otherwise. Their greatest mediums revered their God-given gift too deeply to prostitute it in the marketplace for money. They left that sort of thing to renegade mediums such as Houdini. But in their heart of hearts the spiritualists prayed for a champion to come forward and confound all sceptics by proving beyond doubt that the dead could speak with the living. Although they did not as yet know it such a champion was waiting in the shadows, about to emerge into the light.

She was known as Margery and she was one of the most brilliant mediums in the history of spiritualism. She came just when she was needed, as though divinely sent. Her real name was Mina Crandon. She was the wife of a distinguished Boston surgeon, Dr Le Roi Goddard Crandon, who had taught surgery at Harvard Medical School and was the author of a standard textbook on surgical after-treatment. In May 1923, when his wife's mediumship began, he was fifty years old. Mina at twenty-six was much younger and not quite of his social standing, her first husband having kept a grocery store. She was very attractive; a natural blonde with blue eyes, infectious laugh and a marvellous figure. She was charming, clever, and vivacious. Never was a medium so life-enhancing. When she entered a room she brought with her an aura of warmth, sex, and desire. Men found her irresistible. She was an enchantress.

The Crandons entered fully into the social life of Boston, entertaining a great deal at their gracious house in Lime Street. Crandon was an omnivorous reader and in the spring of 1923 he was reading deeply into spiritualism and psychic research. The subject had become his main interest outside his professional work. Mina became interested and this led her to attend a seance in Boston. The medium went into a trance and said that a spirit was present giving the name of Walter and claiming to be her brother. Mina had a brother called Walter, five years her senior, who had been killed in a railroad accident ten years previously. The spirit of Walter gave her much evidential detail of their childhood together. At the end of the seance the medium asked Mina if she was aware that she was a potential psychic of great power.

Mina told her husband of this and he arranged a trial seance at their home for themselves and four friends. They sat round in a circle and rested their hands on the table. The table moved. From this simple beginning were to develop some of the most extraordinary manifestations ever witnessed in a seance room. Each successive seance was more wonderful than the last. There were materialisations, bugle calls from invisible instruments, clairvoyance, and evidential messages. Live pigeons appeared, either spontaneously created or having passed through matter. Every phenomenon claimed for other mediums she could do and more. Never had there been such manifestations of ectoplasm, that mysterious, protoplasmic substance which streams out of the bodies of mediums and shapes itself into corporeal forms. Ectoplasmic limbs extruded from the orifices of her body and performed all manner of actions—touching people, lifting and throwing objects, overturning tables, and ringing a bell.

All the seances were private, only friends were invited and

they were asked to be discreet; the Crandons wanted no publicity. But news of this great new medium spread through informed circles, and famous spiritualists made the pilgrimage to Boston to have the honour of sitting with her. Their reports circulated throughout the movement, spreading the good news that a brilliant star had arisen.

Only one thing could be said to mar the perfection of the seances and that was the nature of the spirit who controlled Mina and by whom all the phenomena were made possible. The spirit was that of her brother Walter, and he was, to put it mildly, something of an embarrassment. Walter was a rough diamond. His voice was loud and raucous, his language coarse and frequently profane. He was ill-natured and sarcastic. He often shocked the sitters. It was a disconcerting experience to sit in the dark and hear such utterances coming through the lips of the beautiful woman. Another aspect of the seances that some sitters found shocking, though in a different way, was Mina's preference for wearing nothing but a silk kimono, which she usually discarded in the pitch darkness, conducting the seance completely naked.

In the autumn of 1923 news of Mina Crandon reached J. Malcolm Bird, associate editor of *Scientific American* and secretary to the investigating committee. Bird was anxious for good mediums to try for the awards in order to give some standing to the investigation, which had so far failed dismally to attract anyone of merit. He went to Boston to try to persuade Mina to appear before the committee. He had to consult her husband as well, because no seance took place unless Crandon was present. Neither of them was keen on the idea. They told Bird that they did not care for publicity and he returned disappointed to New York. In December Crandon took his wife to Europe, where she baffled eminent scientists in France and England. Doyle and his wife attended one of her seances. There were some flowers on the mantelpiece when the seance began. When it ended the flowers were found at Lady Doyle's feet, an uncharacteristically gracious gesture from Walter.

When the Crandons returned from Europe, Bird tried again to persuade them. This time they agreed, subject to certain conditions. The sittings were to be held in Boston for the convenience of Crandon, whose professional engagements did not permit him easily to come to New York. Also it must be announced in *Scientific American* that Mina was not interested in the money but in the cause of spiritualism. And lastly that her identity should be concealed as long as possible. Bird agreed and he gave her the name 'Margery'.

He thought it best that at first a sub-committee should attend the seances as often as they thought necessary to reach some preliminary conclusions. If these were satisfactory then the full committee would be summoned. This arrangement made a lot of sense. It was hardly worth troubling the full committee if the investigation did not prove worthwhile. He knew from past experience how difficult it was to get them all together. The academics had their commitments and Houdini was usually away on tour. Since Professors McDougall and Comstock were available they were appointed as the sub-committee. Hereward Carrington attended several seances and so did Dr Walter Franklin Prince. As for Bird, he was hardly ever away from Boston.

The seances began in April 1924. The hospitable Crandons always invited members of the committee to stay at their Lime Street home. Bird always did and so did Carrington. Bird stayed so often that he became almost one of the family. He attended all the seances. Not being a member of the committee he was never one of the circle of sitters, but he appointed himself to a special role outside the circle. Crandon always controlled, that is held, Margery's right hand; another sitter controlled her left. The seances took place in total darkness, so as to prevent any collusion between Crandon and his wife. Bird controlled their link with his right hand, leaving his left hand free to explore Margery's body in order to detect movements that might be regarded as suspicious, or to locate any articles that she might have concealed after the lights were out. It was later said that Bird had given himself the choicest role in the investigation. The extent of his explorations in the pitch dark could not be determined, but the proximity of the lovely medium, her naked state, and the friendliness of her disposition, led to the irresistible conclusion that Bird's exploring hand sometimes went further than science demanded.

Certainly Bird became convinced of the genuineness of Margery's mediumship and so did Carrington. Houdini knew nothing of her until he read in the New York *Times* of the marvellous Boston medium who was baffling members of the committee. By this time he was the only member of the committee who had not sat with her. He stormed into the office of Orson D. Munn, proprietor of *Scientific American,* demanding an explanation. Bird was called in and explained the arrangements he had made, saying that no final verdict would be decided on Margery until the full committee had sat with her. So what was the nature of Houdini's complaint? Houdini could not tell him that it seemed that his great fear since joining the committee was about to be realised. He was now the declared enemy of the spiritualists, declaring all mediums to be fakes. If his distinguished colleagues endorsed Margery he would be a laughing stock, all reputation gone. The spiritualists would have the victory.

His fear was well-founded. Bird told him that although McDougall, Comstock, and Prince were still non-committal he had little doubt that they would give her the award. He himself believed her to be genuine and so did Carrington. Houdini was most disturbed and questioned him further. When he learned that both Bird and Carrington had accepted the hospitality of the Crandons he exploded again. Bird was not a member of the committee, but Carrington was. How could he be impartial when he had stayed as a guest? In this he found an ally in Dr Prince, who argued that it would be embarrassing to expose a person whose hospitality one had enjoyed, and even more embarrassing in the event of a favourable verdict to incur the imputation that friendship had affected the decision.

Having brought Carrington's impartiality into question, Houdini demanded that some sittings with Margery be arranged for him immediately. She agreed to sit on 23 and 24 July. When Houdini set off for Boston Munn thought it best to go with him. The reputation of his periodical was at stake and Houdini was so angry that Munn feared what he would do in Boston. For it was obvious that Houdini was not going into these seances with scientific detachment. He had already decided that Margery was a fraud and he intended to expose her quickly, damagingly, and with the maximum publicity.

Margery awaited them in Boston, beautiful, seductive, and welcoming. She invited them to stay in her home, but Houdini led Munn off to an hotel. The first of the two seances was held at the Crandons' home. Before the seance began, the room was thoroughly searched by Houdini. Margery had made it clear that she would not submit to an internal examination by a doctor or nurse, otherwise she was willing to be searched. Since she was wearing next to nothing this was considered unnecessary.

They sat round a table on which was placed a megaphone. The light was switched off. Crandon controlled Margery's right hand, and Bird, as usual, controlled this link with his right hand, leaving his exploring hand free. Houdini controlled Margery's left hand and also controlled her foot by pressing his right ankle against her left ankle. She pressed back, flirtatiously it seemed, but he suspected that she was increasing the pressure so that should she move her leg away the tactile impression that it was still against his would remain. He was prepared for any movement of her leg. All that day he had worn a tight elastic bandage round his right calf. He had removed this just before the seance and now his lower leg was so swollen and tender that the lightest movement against it would be felt. To exploit its sensitivity to the full he had, under the cover of darkness, rolled up his trouser leg above the knee. A bell-box had been placed between his feet. This contained an electric bell which was activated by depressing a wooden flap on the top of the box. The bell-box was one of Walter's favourite gadgets; he loved to make the bell ring.

After a few minutes of silence Walter's voice came through the pitch darkness, brash, slangy, uncouth and profane. He welcomed Houdini to the proceedings and touched him several times on the inside of his right leg. At least Walter said that it was he who was doing this; Houdini had his doubts. What he had no doubts about at all was that Margery's left foot had begun to move slowly, very, very slowly. Her leg was sliding gently, ever so gently, against his sensitive calf. She was stretching it out until her toe could touch the bell-box lid. Suddenly the bell rang, and he felt her leg moving back to its original position.

Walter expressed his pleasure with the way things were going and then asked Bird to fetch a plaque from the other side of the room. While Bird was doing this the link between Crandon and Margery was unguarded. Walter shouted to Houdini to control Margery. Houdini grabbed her right hand. Walter then informed the company that the megaphone was no longer on the table but was floating in the air. He asked Houdini where he should throw it. Houdini asked for it to be thrown in his direction and the megaphone landed at his feet.

When the seance was over, Houdini told Munn and Bird how Margery had rung the bell. He also gave them his explanation of the megaphone phenomenon. When Bird released the hands of Crandon and Margery, and before he himself had hold of both her hands, she had quickly picked up the megaphone, and inverted it on her head like a dunce's cap. When he had asked for the megaphone to be thrown towards him, she had simply jerked her head in his direction so that the megaphone landed near him. This meant that she worked in collusion with her husband. And although he said nothing about it at the time, Houdini was beginning to suspect that Bird was part of the act.

The second seance took place the following evening at Professor Comstock's apartment in Beacon Street. Again Houdini controlled Margery's left hand while Crandon controlled her right, and again Bird, outside the circle, controlled the Crandon-Margery link. The door was locked, the lights switched off, and the seance began. Houdini felt a tap on his right knee and Walter said, 'Ha, ha, Houdini'. Then he felt the table begin to move, sometimes towards him, sometimes away from him. It leaned up against him on two legs and dropped back again. He released his left hand, which Munn was holding, and probed gently under the table. It came into contact with Margery's head. He realised that by leaning forward in her chair she had got her head under the table and was moving it from side to side and up and down. Finally, with a jerk of her head, she tipped the table right up and over. This violent overturning of the table startled the rest of the sitters, who ascribed it to an astonishing manifestation of Walter's choleric nature.

After the seance Houdini, Munn, Comstock and Bird withdrew to another room. Houdini told them what he had discovered and asked whether he should expose Margery on the spot. But the others agreed with Bird's suggestion that the full committee should meet before making any statement. Houdini and Munn returned to New York. Bird stayed on in Boston as a guest of the Crandons. He told them what Houdini had discovered. Houdini had been right in his suspicion. Bird, who had first come to Boston as the loyal secretary to the committee, was now a creature of the Crandons, utterly bewitched by Margery.

A second series of sittings was organised for August as an attempt to get a final verdict from the full committee. It had been difficult to find dates that suited all the members. Prince and Comstock had promised to attend. McDougall could not be located, so it had been decided to proceed without him. Carrington had withdrawn from further sittings, having pronounced his belief in the genuineness of Margery's mediumship. Houdini was on the road in vaudeville until his next lecture tour began in the autumn, but he had vowed that he would attend the seances no matter how many bookings he had to cancel.

In the planning of the seances there were some important changes in procedure. Crandon would not be allowed to control his wife's right hand. To control her more securely Houdini and his assistant, James Collins, had devised a cabinet. This was a wooden box, in shape a cross between an upright piano and a slant-topped desk. There was space enough inside for Margery to sit comfortably. In the lid was a hole for her neck and in the sides two holes, one for each arm. When Margery entered the cabinet, she would be totally enclosed except for her head and her arms. The third change, insisted upon by Houdini, was that Bird should be excluded from all the seances.

The first of the sittings before the full committee took place at Comstock's apartment in Boston on 25 August. Margery was placed in the cabinet and the lid was closed. She thrust her hands through the holes in the sides, Houdini controlled her left hand and Prince her right. The bell-box was placed on the table. No sooner had the lights been switched off than a violent noise was heard. The lights were switched on and it was found that the lid of the cabinet had been thrown back. Houdini maintained that Margery could have thrust it open with her shoulders, although he and also Prince had to admit that they had felt no movement in her hands nor tension in her muscles.

The lid of the cabinet was closed again and the lights were switched off. Walter's voice came through loud and menacing. He addressed himself to Houdini. 'You think you're smart, don't you,' he shouted. 'How much are they paying you for stopping the phenomena here?'

'I don't know what you're talking about,' Houdini retorted. 'It's costing me two thousand and five hundred dollars a week to be here.'

'Where did you turn down a two thousand five hundred dollar a week contract in August?' Walter sneered.

'In Buffalo,' Houdini said.

'You had no work for all this week,' Walter shouted. 'How much are you getting for stopping these phenomena?'

Professor Comstock intervened. 'What do you mean by this, Walter?' he asked. 'This isn't psychic research.'

'Comstock,' Walter said, in a voice shaking with rage, 'You take that bell-box out into a good light, examine it and report back. You'll see fast enough what I mean.'

Comstock did as Walter instructed and found, tucked down into the angle between the flap and the top of the box, a rubber eraser off the end of a pencil. While this did not make the bell wholly inoperative, he estimated that four times the usual amount of pressure was now needed to ring it. Crandon accused Houdini of tampering with the bell-box in order to discredit his wife. Houdini swore that he had done no such thing. The seance broke off in confusion. After these extraordinary scenes, the academics on the committee had grave reservations about Houdini's fitness to investigate psychic phenomena. A slanging-match and possible punch-up between him and the disembodied Walter was the last thing they had expected. They looked forward to the next seance with some trepidation.

Before the seance the following night, Bird approached Houdini and demanded to know why he was being excluded. Houdini gave it to him straight, telling him that he didn't know how to keep his mouth shut. Bird admitted that he was at fault, that he had tried to keep quiet about Houdini's discoveries at the previous seances, but Margery had wheedled them out of him. He then resigned as secretary to the committee.

To prevent the lid of the cabinet opening as it had done the previous night, Houdini and Collins had added padlocks, staples, and hasps. Margery entered the cabinet and was locked in. Again her hands were controlled through the holes in the sides. The lights were switched off and Walter came thundering through, his voice crackling with anger. He swore fearfully at Houdini, calling down curses on his head. On being asked what was amiss, he said that a ruler had been left in the cabinet by Collins in another attempt to discredit Margery. Then he returned to his reviling of Houdini. He called him a bastard and a god-damned son of a bitch. He told him to get the hell out and never come back, for if he didn't he himself certainly would.

The lights were switched on and the cabinet opened. On the floor near Margery's feet was a folded carpenter's ruler, seven inches long but capable of being extended to two feet. If Margery's hands had been inside the cabinet, and at a later stage of the seance they could have been, she could have manipulated the ruler through the neck hole and, by holding it in her teeth, rung the bell-box on the table in front of the cabinet. Collins came in and swore that he had not put the ruler in the cabinet. Then Houdini swore a sacred oath on the memory of his sainted mother that he too knew nothing of the matter. Again the seance was discontinued, and the bemused academics reflected on how humdrum their lives had been until they had gone investigating the spirit world with Houdini.

Before the last sitting on the following night, Margery told Houdini that she hoped he would not denounce her publicly in Boston, as she believed it was his intention to do, for if this were to happen her friends were sure to beat him up. Then Crandon took him to one side and jovially suggested that if he could only be converted to a belief in his wife's mediumship he would gladly donate ten thousand dollars to any charity Houdini cared to name. Houdini received both remarks in stony silence. He had no sympathy for either of the Crandons.

They were indeed a strange pair. In public their behaviour was impeccable, but there were rumours of bizarre activities in private. Crandon was widely respected as a brilliant surgeon, but no one could make him out as a person. His true role in his wife's mediumship can only be guessed at. It is certainly suggestive that the deeper he read into psychic matters the more adept she became. It was noticeable that he was keener on the seances than she was. Throughout that hot summer, while Houdini and the rest of the committee investigated her, she had complained of having to sit in hot, stuffy rooms and had talked of picnics and sailing. Crandon had been the one who insisted on the seances; he so obviously wanted to show off his wife's powers. He always called her Psyche, never Mina or Margery, and spoke of Walter as though he lived just around the corner.

The committee assembled for the final seance. The lights were switched off and developments were awaited. But Walter was subdued and no bells rang. It only remained for the committee to ponder on all they had witnessed concerning Margery. They were critical of her, but they also privately voiced their regret over Houdini's behaviour. As the seances continued, they had become increasingly doubtful of his scrupulosity and impartiality. This made it especially difficult for them to evaluate the incidents of the eraser and the ruler. It would seem that enclosing Margery in the cabinet had prevented her producing any effects and that she and her husband had, therefore, good cause to introduce these objects, and by throwing the blame on Houdini provide reasons for the lack of phenomena. On the other hand, Houdini's hostility and obvious intention of proving her a fraud put them in the invidious position of having to consider that he had been the one responsible for placing the objects where they had been found.

In the event, Margery did not win the *Scientific American*

award. Only Carrington believed her to be genuine. Comstock did not think that rigid proof had been furnished. McDougall was inclined to regard all the phenomena as produced by normal means. Prince found her unconvincing. Each in his different way hinted at deception. Houdini did not qualify his judgment in the slightest. He stated that everything that had taken place at the seances had been a deliberate and conscious fraud. So far as he was concerned, Margery, who had been described as the brightest star in the spiritualist firmament, had not been dimmed but totally extinguished.

Chapter Ten

HOUDINI IS DOOMED

Margery had been exposed. Houdini left no one in doubt about that. From the Pacific coast to the Atlantic, he lectured on the Boston seances and distributed a pamphlet he had written, which emphasised his leading role in the affair. He was the scourge of all mediums. They hated and feared him. They did all they could to discredit him. They said that he was an alcoholic, a drug addict, a notorious womaniser; that he had sold his soul to the Devil; that he was in the pay of the Pope; that he was the secret agent of a Jewish conspiracy to undermine the Christian faith. They claimed that he was harassing not so much them as the immortal spirits, and that a dreadful retribution was inevitable. So let him continue to rave like a madman, for the shadows were thickening quickly around him. In December Walter predicted that he had less than a year to live.

On 2 January 1925 Houdini was back in Boston to give a lecture at the Symphony Hall, where Doyle had given his lecture. Earlier in the day he had gone to City Hall, where, watched by a great crowd, he had walked up the steps to deposit with the Mayor the five thousand dollars he would give to any Boston medium, Margery included, who could produce phenomena he could not duplicate. That night he told his audience of his sittings with Margery and how he had caught her cheating. He denounced Carrington and Bird, saying that they were in league with the Crandons. Then he asked two members of the audience to come on to the platform. He made one sit on his left and the other on his right. He placed dark hoods over their heads to simulate the conditions in the seance room. He asked them to control his hands and feet, and then he showed all the tricks Margery had played. He put his head under the table and the table rocked from side to side and levitated until there were only two legs on the floor. He tossed the megaphone and rang the bell-box. The two sitters were mystified by all this, for they believed they had him securely controlled. The audience, who could see everything, roared with laughter. He brought on the cabinet designed to enclose Margery, and sitting in it he manoeuvred a two foot rule through the neck hole, and then, holding it in his teeth, he made the bell-box ring. The audience gave him an ovation and he left Boston in triumph.

But as fast as he solved one mystery he was faced with another. It was as though he were locked in a cell within a cell, within a cell, *ad infinitum,* never to break free. Reports were coming from England that Gilbert Murray, Regius Professor of Greek at Oxford and past president of the British Society for Psychical Research, together with the Earl of Balfour, also a past president of the society, had completed two hundred and fifty-nine experiments in thought transference, with positive results. The procedure had been that Murray and a group of friends first gathered in a room. Then Murray went out while a subject was decided on. This was announced aloud by a person acting as spokesman for the group, so that all the members would have it clearly fixed in their minds. Murray then returned and attempted to mentally visualise the subject on which the group were concentrating.

The subjects were not simple but complex. In one test the group were thinking of Gladstone summoning Lloyd George to 10 Downing Street and pointing out the indiscretions in a speech he had recently made in Paris. Murray entered the room and said that he could see a dignified man severely reproving some-one—giving him an awful dressing down. He thought it was Gladstone—it was something political. He couldn't think whom Gladstone would be likely to rebuke—oh, he was rebuking Lloyd George. In another test the group concentrated on the sinking of the *Titanic,* and one of the bandsmen playing 'Nearer My God to Thee,' and then diving off and sitting on his cello until picked up by a boat. Murray said that he could see something awful—a shipwreck—the *Lusitania*—no, not the *Lusitania*—the one that ran into an iceberg—the *Titanic*—and the singing of a hymn. He felt as if somebody was crashing a fiddle or cello, or breaking it up. He could see people being picked up out of the water and being saved.

Such results were inexplicable. It seemed that at last mental telepathy had been proved. Houdini did not agree; in his opinion Murray's experiments were fraudulent. Yet it was hard to accuse any members of the group of collusion. In the course of the experiments, thirty-six people had at different times been the spokesman and about twenty others had been present on different occasions. Moreover, the world would hardly believe that so famous a scholar as Murray could stoop to fraud, yet as Houdini reflected, a distinguished Boston surgeon had done exactly that.

He did not understand what twist in the minds of such brilliant men led them to cheat. It was not a criminal urge; they made no money from it. Perhaps they were over-educated and the rigorous mental discipline practised over many years eventually repelled them, so that the desire to cheat overcame their dedication to the truth. Then they would find great satisfaction in using their superior intellects to put one over on their fellow men, to play their own hidden game, to indulge in secret laughter and contempt. It could be that they longed to prove the unprovable, desired so much for a thing to be true that they set about making it so. He did not know, but of one thing he was certain; whatever the explanation of Murray's experiments it was definitely not telepathy. The great stage mentalists, Robert Heller among them, had made a lifelong study of the subject and none of them had ever claimed telepathic power. Why then should this power manifest itself in some professor of Greek playing weekend parlour games at Oxford?

So right from the start, as with Margery, he had decided that Murray was a fraud. Even before he had looked into the matter, he had already reached his conclusion. His fellow members of the *Scientific American* committee had been right to doubt his impartiality. He who had been denied communication with his mother would not allow that supernatural or even paranormal mysteries could take place this side of the grave. It was true that he believed it to be his sacred duty to prevent anyone indulging in the same false hopes as he had done. But it was also true that bitterness, rage, and frustration informed his crusade. Other people's hopes, like his, must be dashed. He could not bear the thought that what had been denied to him might have been granted to others; and that was why he could never allow a medium to be declared genuine or a mystery left unsolved.

He stated that he would solve the mystery of Murray's experiments by duplicating them himself. Murray's group had always been distinguished, so Houdini gathered in his home some of the most eminent people in New York, among them Ralph Pulitzer, publisher of the New York *World,* Bernard M. Baruch, former chairman of the War Industries Board, and Dr Edward J. Kempf, a psychiatrist. The group also included his brother Dash. Houdini was escorted upstairs to a small bedroom and one of the group guarded the door. Two floors below, Dr Kempf chose a subject and Dash, as spokesman, repeated it to the whole group.

Houdini returned to the room and swayed visibly backward at the vivid mental image of black oxen stampeding. He saw a man, a hungry man, sitting on a horse. He was chasing the oxen—no, they weren't oxen, they were buffaloes. The man was shooting at them—he had long hair and piercing eyes. No, the group weren't thinking of the man, but of his statue. The man was Buffalo Bill. They were thinking of his statue in Wyoming and the sculptor. This had indeed been the subject. The next test was even more difficult. When he came into the room, he visualised Shakespeare's home at Stratford-upon-Avon and a large audience —but these seemed to be in America. There was a theatrical family who came from England—the Barrymores—possibly John Barrymore. Houdini hadn't got it quite right. The group had been thinking of Ethel Barrymore. In another test he visualised a huge body that heaved and swayed—an enormous body of water and a lot of shipwrecks. The group had been concentrating on the phrase 'Don't give up the ship.'

The group was baffled. Houdini told them that there had been no telepathy. He had done what he had done by trickery. He refused to say more than that. He had proved that he could duplicate Murray's experiments and, so far as he was concerned, that was an end to the matter. He left it to more judicious minds than his to point out that the duplication of phenomena did not necessarily invalidate it. The world would know what he wanted it to know; that another fraud had been exposed, that Houdini had done it again.

How had he done it? Simply by hiding a dictaphone in the room. No member of the group expected this; the instrument was a recent invention and the bugging of rooms had not yet become an everyday occurrence. Dash had been near the microphone when he announced the subjects and Houdini had heard him on the receiver in the bedroom. He had not revealed this secret to the group because he was not yet ready to share it. The dictaphone remained in place, another addition to the trap doors, sliding panels, and secret hiding places that made his home a house of magic. Through it he would listen to visitors gathered in the room below, and then descend to astound them with his omniscience.

*

He was anxious to intensify his crusade against the mediums, but he was short of money. So he decided to return to vaudeville in order to raise a fighting fund. On 12 January 1925 he began a short season at the New York Hippodrome. During his lecture tours he had become aware of the entertainment value of exposing mediums' tricks onstage. He incorporated some of these into his repertoire and found himself with the most sensational act in vaudeville.

A committee from the audience sat hooded on the stage, controlling his hands and feet, bewildered by the phenomena all around them. The person with his foot planted firmly on Houdini's shoe could not know that the shoe was a trick one from which he could easily withdraw his foot. The audience could see, what the committee could not, that Houdini's sock was cut short to expose the toes and with these he picked up a tambourine some distance away from him and rattled it merrily. He repeated all of Margery's tricks, tilting the table, throwing the megaphone, and ringing the bell.

When his season at the Hippodrome ended, he left for a five month vaudeville tour on the Keith circuit. Another stage of his crusade had begun. In vaudeville he could reach more people; he could entertain and expose at the same time; and he could also raise the money to finance his campaign. He used the money to form a group of psychic investigators, who went ahead of him, attended seances, and were ready with evidence of fraud when he arrived. Then these local mediums would be denounced from the stage. He would challenge them to come up beside him and produce psychic phenomena that he could not duplicate. He told his audience that he was offering a stake of five thousand dollars. Why then were there never any takers? The mediums said that they couldn't produce phenomena to order, that the spirits wouldn't come just like that for money. How then did these same mediums, under their own conditions, produce regular manifestations for a two dollar fee? Sometimes the mediums among the audience would stand up to defend themselves. Then he would have a spotlight turned on them so that the audience could clearly see at whom he was pointing an accusing finger. To the audiences all this was superb, unique, first-class entertainment; to the spiritualists it was blasphemy.

He did not confine his exposures to the vaudeville stage. Sometimes, when primed of fraud, he would attend a seance disguised behind a beard and thick spectacles, and accompanied by a local detective and newspaper reporter. He made a special point of attending trumpet seances. As soon as the lights were extinguished, he would reach for the trumpet and smear it with lamp black. Then the trumpet would float in the darkness while spirits played celestial melodies upon it. When the lights went up, the medium's hands and mouth were found to be smudged with lampblack. The detective would arrest the medium, and the presence of the reporter would ensure a front page story the following day.

Over in England Doyle was distressed when he read reports of

Houdini's activities. It seemed to him that his erstwhile friend didn't care that he was bringing ruin and disgrace to genuine mediums; that he would do anything to focus attention on himself. In the garish lights of vaudeville he was hounding and baiting God's elect for money and personal publicity. In Doyle's eyes, Houdini had become a persecutor. Terrible as this was, Doyle had a greater concern; he feared for Houdini's soul. Mediums were prophesying the death of Houdini; his days were numbered. Doyle prayed that he would see the light before it was too late.

In April Houdini celebrated his fifty-first birthday. His friends noticed that he looked exhausted. Yet never had he been so busy. He was engaged in many public controversies, he dealt with an enormous correspondence, and although heavily committed in vaudeville he rarely refused an invitation to lecture. Later in the month he lectured at the New York Police Academy on how to catch fake mediums. Young trainees listened agog as he advised them not to grab the ectoplasm from the front but to grab it from behind, and then they would get the medium too. He was recognised internationally as the man the mediums feared most, and yet in his heart he still yearned to believe that spiritualism was true. The need to talk to his mother, to find out her final message, still obsessed him. He had to know. The turmoil in his mind never ceased. Fears for his sanity continued to oppress him. Sometimes he visited as many as three lunatic asylums in one week.

In among all his activities he was working on the arrangements for a national tour in the autumn with a full scale magic show. He was no longer concerned about the competition of Thurston. His show would be unique. He planned it in three parts. In the first he would perform magic, the sort of magic that had fascinated him since he was a boy. In the second he would perform his escapes. And in the third he would duplicate psychic phenomena and expose mediums.

In September 1925 he took his show on the road, and wherever he played it was a triumph. He opened with magic. He covered a glowing lamp with a silk handkerchief, and when this was

F

whisked away the lamp was gone. He turned a beautiful girl into a rosebush. Cards and coins appeared and vanished at his finger-tips. He produced rabbits out of the air and also a glass bowl, brimful of water and filled with live gold fish. He performed his tricks simply and directly, more in the manner of an expert giving a demonstration than a stage magician. He had no patter like Thurston. The phrase, 'Will wonders never cease,' which he used at the end of each trick was delivered in an off-hand manner, a perfunctory concession to a theatrical convention.

Like Thurston he was surrounded by beautiful girls, who acted as his assistants, but when he performed Metamorphosis he brought Bess onstage and introduced her as the girl he had been travelling with for thirty-one years. In the second part he featured his repertoire of escapes, freeing himself from trunks, coffins, or whatever took his fancy that particular night; but he always closed with the Torture Cell.

The third part of the show, with its revelations of the methods of spook crooks, was the greatest hit of the evening. Wherever he went, he challenged the local mediums to come up on to the stage. He had raised his offer to ten thousand dollars. Although he had never yet been duped by a medium, he lived in constant terror that this could happen and he would be made to look ridiculous. This dread gave his performance an edge, a nervous excitement, which communicated itself to the audience.

His team of investigators, which already numbered a dozen, had been considerably strengthened by Rose Mackenberg, a pri-vate detective, who was as dedicated to the exposure of fraud as he was. In December, in Worcester, a man from the audience shouted that Christ had been persecuted and now the spiritualists were being persecuted. Houdini shouted back that Christ had never robbed people of two dollars, the going rate for a seance in Worcester. Then he asked for a spotlight to be directed at one of the stage boxes. There the audience saw a mysterious figure, a woman dressed all in black, with a veil covering her face. He introduced her as Rose Mackenberg, a member of his staff. He told them that on that day, that very day, for the payment of thirteen dollars, that was all, with no theological qualifications whatsoever, she had been ordained a minister of Worcester's Unity Spiritualist Church, empowered to conduct seances and bring back to earth the spirits of the dead. Raising his fists to heaven, he vowed that he would never rest until he had exposed every fake medium in every state in America.

What a show! The audience were watching a man whom they could no longer define. Who was he? A magician, an escape artist, the greatest star in vaudeville, the scourge of the mediums. Yes, but he was more, much more than all of these. He was a legend, a symbol, a myth . . . he was Houdini.

*

His work of cleansing the country of spook crooks continued. Rose Mackenberg and his team of investigators had reported that Washington was the worst spot in the country for these fakers. Unlike most states, the District of Columbia had no law against fortune-telling, and as a result the capital of the nation swarmed with them. Some exerted such power that Senators and Representatives were being guided by them in shaping and passing legislation. There was reason to believe that not even the occupants of the White House were immune from their influence. Mrs Harding, wife of the late President, had consulted mediums regularly. One had prophesied that her husband would become President, and another had seen the Star of Destiny burning upon his forehead, the star that would guide her illustrious husband to glory. As things turned out, it guided him to preside over the most flagrantly corrupt administration in the history of America.

Houdini set about the task of ridding Washington of this pestilence of spook crooks. He persuaded Representative Sol Bloom, of New York State, to introduce a bill forbidding fortune-telling in the District of Columbia under a penalty of two hundred and fifty dollars fine, or six months in prison, or both. On 26 February 1926 the bill came up for hearing before a House of Representatives committee and Houdini travelled to Washington to testify. The public gallery was crowded with mediums, palm readers, astrologers, crystal gazers and lucky charm sellers, all sending a wave of hate across the room to where he was sitting.

One medium and then another testified to the committee that they had frequently been consulted by Senators and Representatives to whom the spirits had given a guiding hand. They refused to break the secrecy of the seance room and name names, but they assured the committee that the spirits had given excellent advice, from which the country had benefited considerably. This caused quite a stir. The following day the New York *Times* demanded further questioning and insisted on the disclosure of these legislative clients. People began to wonder whether the present incumbent of the White House was as susceptible to spirit influences as his predecessor. Calvin Coolidge had a calming influence on the nation. He believed that the least government was the best government, and in pursuit of this ideal he dozed each afternoon in his rocking chair on the White House porch in full view of the crowds in Pennsylvania Avenue. These had always tended to view their sleeping President with pride, as an indication of the stability and well-being of the country, but now they had cause to wonder whether he was napping or in a trance-like state communing with the spirits.

When Houdini took the stand, he gave his occupation as author, psychic investigator, and mysterious entertainer. In his evidence he gave details of his investigations, saying that in thirty-five years he had never found a genuine medium and now did not believe that one existed. All the mediums he had encountered were of two kinds, mental degenerates and deliberate cheats. They extorted millions of dollars each year and the government did nothing about it. The spook crooks in the public gallery murmured angrily. He took a telegram from his pocket, crumpled it and threw it towards them, challenging any of them to read the contents. They were silent. He challenged any of them to tell him the name his mother had called him when he was a little child. Again they were silent.

A member of the committee asked him if he had psychic powers. Houdini said that he had not. Another member asked him if he could prove this. Houdini didn't reply. The committee pressed him on this point, asking that if he did not dematerialise himself then how did he get out of the Torture Cell. All he would say was that he did it as anyone else would do it.

Mrs Jane B. Coates, the best-known medium in Washington, took the stand. She was asked to define the word 'mystic'. She said that a mystic was a person who had evoked certain senses within themselves which brought them knowledge from the world beyond. Asked whether Houdini was a mystic, she said that he was one of the greatest mystics in the world.

The hearing was adjourned until 18 May, and when it was resumed Houdini continued his attack on the mediums. He produced a 'spirit' voice from a trumpet without moving his lips and caused a message to appear on a blank slate. The mediums, in turn, attacked him when they took the stand. They questioned his morals and his sanity; they called him vile and crazy. He demanded the right to rebut these charges. When this was granted, he surprised everyone by asking for Bess to be placed on the stand.

He said that he wanted the chairman to see her. He told him that the following month Bess and he would celebrate their thirty-second wedding anniversary. He said that there were no medals or ribbons pinned on him, but when a girl would stick to a man for thirty-two years as she had done, when she would starve with him and work with him through thick and thin, then that was a pretty good recommendation. He said that outside his mother Bess had been his greatest friend. Turning to her, he asked if he had ever shown traces of being crazy unless it was about her. She smiled and said no. He asked her if he had ever been brutal to her or vile. She smiled and said no. He asked her if he was a good boy. She smiled and said yes.

Rosabelle, sweet Rosabelle, I love you more than I can tell. Thirty-two years ago, at Coney Island, she had stood with him at midnight on a lonely bridge over dark running water, when he had raised her hand to heaven and asked her to swear that she would never betray him. Now he had made a public acknowledgment of her steadfastness and declared his love for her. His words had been taken down by the assembled reporters to be read next day all over America. They had been taken down by the court stenographer to be recorded and deposited in the archives of Congress, there to remain as long as the United States should exist. So did Houdini declare his love for Bess.

The hearings ended on 21 May. No law was passed. The proposed bill failed on the technical grounds that as worded it would have been too difficult to enforce. Houdini had lost this fight and the spook crooks rejoiced.

He had lost and he was tired, very tired. Yet he intensified his crusade and, in addition, he was planning an even bigger magic show for the autumn. He never rested; there was still so much he had to do. He wanted to establish a University of Magic, and had already planned the curriculum. He never ceased learning. He had always been conscious of his lack of formal education and that summer he intended taking courses in English at Columbia University. Then there was the idea he had been working on since filming *The Man from Beyond;* to really have himself frozen into a block of ice and then escape from it. So far he had been unable to solve the problem, but developments in quick refrigeration were pointing the way. He wanted to introduce the escape the following year. Looking further ahead, he wanted to be nailed in a box, which would be swept over the Niagara Falls and smashed to splinters in the whirlpool below. Then he would appear mysteriously on the shore.

But while Houdini made these plans, the spirits were poised to thwart him. Walter told the Crandons that he had little time left to live. Over in England, Doyle, in his home circle, had a message, 'Houdini is doomed, doomed, doomed!' So seriously did Doyle take the warning that he would have written to Houdini, but he knew that his words would have no effect, that Houdini would only have mocked at them. So all Doyle could do was to follow Houdini's every move and wait for the inevitable coming of the Angel of Death.

Chapter Eleven

THE ULTIMATE ESCAPE

That summer, tired as he was, Houdini went into battle again. Rahman Bey, a twenty-six year old 'Egyptian Miracle Worker', had recently arrived in America to give demonstrations of mind over matter. He was sponsored by Hereward Carrington, the only member of the *Scientific American* committee to endorse Margery. Rahman Bey thrust needles through his cheeks and skewers through the flesh of his chest; lay flat on a bed of nails while an assistant stood on his stomach; and allowed a stone slab to be hammered to pieces on his chest as he rested on the upturned blades of swords. But Houdini was not concerned with these tricks; he knew them too well from his dime museum days. Sticking needles and skewers through flesh did not hurt when done quickly; on the bed of nails, the nails were too close to penetrate; and the sword blades on which Rahman Bey rested so easily were too blunt to cut butter. But there was one trick that Houdini could not explain.

Rahman Bey went into a trance, standing with his hands over his face. Then he fell back rigid into the arms of two assistants. They placed his body in a zinc coffin, bolted the lid and soldered it. Then they covered the coffin with sand until it was completely buried. While this was going on, Carrington was telling the audience of Rahman Bey's power to slow down his respiration and circulation until these almost stopped, thus bringing about a state which could only be described as living death. According to medical opinion, there was barely enough air in the coffin to last three minutes, but ten minutes were allowed to elapse before the sand was shovelled away. The coffin was opened and the Egyptian rose unsteadily to his feet.

Remarkable as this was, Carrington promised that Rahman Bey would perform a feat even more astonishing; he would be sealed in a bronze coffin and lowered several fathoms into the Hudson River. There he would remain for one hour. On the day a great crowd assembled. The coffin containing the Egyptian was about to disappear beneath the surface, when the electric emergency bell, which connected him with his assistants on the pier, rang insistently. The coffin was hastily raised and the lid ripped open. Inside lay the Egyptian still in a trance. When he revived, he denied all knowledge of having rung the bell. Carrington's explanation was that Rahman Bey had inadvertently rolled over on to the bell and the weight of his body had caused it to ring. Houdini, who knew better than most the fearful sensation of being lowered into deep, dark waters, believed that the Egyptian's courage had failed him. Certainly Rahman Bey played it safer in his repeat attempt, which took place at the Dalton swimming pool on Fifty-ninth Street. This time he stayed in the coffin for one hour.

The achievement was headline news. The public were now willing to accept Carrington's view that Rahman Bey had supernormal powers. Houdini, when interviewed by reporters, questioned this. He believed that the trick lay in breathing shallowly to conserve the air. Carrington publicly challenged him to duplicate the Egyptian's feat. Houdini accepted the challenge, claiming that he would do it, not by going into a trance or any other kind of hocus-pocus, but simply by natural means.

He had a galvanized iron box built to the measurement of Rahman Bey's coffin—six feet six inches long, twenty-two inches wide, and twenty-two inches high. Inside he installed a telephone and an emergency bell. For three weeks he trained in the basement of his house, not in water but with the lid sealed. On 5 August he gave a public demonstration in the swimming pool of the Shelton Hotel. He wore black swimming trunks and spent some minutes inhaling and exhaling deeply in order to store up a reserve of oxygen. He said that if he died it would be the will of God and his own foolishness. Then he lay down in the box, the lid was soldered, and the box was lowered beneath the surface of the pool.

Joe Rinn, as official timekeeper, called out the time every five minutes. Quarter of an hour passed. Half an hour. Threequarters of an hour. Houdini remained in the box. One hour. He had equalled Rahman Bey's record and still he remained submerged. Now Rinn called out the time every minute. One hour and five minutes. One hour and ten minutes. One hour and a quarter. Suddenly the telephone bell rang. Collins answered it. The crowd waited, expecting the box to be brought to the surface. But Houdini had phoned to say that although the box was leaking he was in no immediate danger. Now Rinn called out the time every thirty seconds. At one and a half hours Houdini phoned again, this time asking to be brought up. The box was hauled out of the pool and opened. He sat up, drained of all energy, soaking wet. A doctor examined him and found his blood pressure 42 compared with 84 when sealed in the box, and his pulse which had been 84 was now 142. The temperature inside the box had reached 99.2 degrees.

Houdini told the reporters that there was nothing remarkable in what he had done; any ordinary person could do the same There was no need to go into a trance. The trick was to breathe shallowly and keep body movement to a minimum. In this way the air in the box had lasted much longer than medical opinion estimated. Of course a steady nerve was needed; any panic would increase the intake of air. He hoped that the knowledge gained through his exploit would be useful to miners and any other workers who were likely to be trapped underground.

He had a bronze coffin made to the same size as the box. It was a beautiful piece of work, magnificent and costly. He announced that he would use it when he performed the feat as a stunt during his autumn tour, but he privately told his friends that it had also been made for his own burial. He had a sense of impending doom. Setting out on his last tour in September 1926, he knew that he was marked for death.

It was as though he had entered a dark tunnel not knowing

when he would see the light at the end, or indeed if there was any end at all. It was all to happen in the month of October. On the 3rd the show opened in Providence. On the 7th Bess was taken very ill. Ptomaine poisoning was diagnosed. Houdini was worried about her. He sent to New York for Sophie Rosenblatt, a nurse who had attended Bess on previous occasions. On the 8th he sat with Bess all night. On the 9th, Saturday, Bess was fit enough to travel with the show to Albany. She now had Nurse Rosenblatt with her and he felt easy enough in his mind to return to New York for a brief business visit.

He caught the last train from Albany, which jolted from stop to stop through the long dark night, preventing him from sleeping. In New York he consulted with his attorney, Bernard Ernst, and visited Martinka's magic shop to purchase some equipment. On the 11th, Monday, he returned to Albany on the early morning train. Then he sat with Bess until it was time to go to the theatre. He had hardly slept for three nights.

In the second part of the show, as he prepared for the Torture Cell Escape, he was overcome by extreme fatigue, but he allowed Collins and Vickery to fasten him in the stocks and haul him up in the air. Suddenly he felt a sharp, scalding pain in his left ankle. He was lowered to the floor and the stocks removed. Collins and Vickery helped him off the stage. There was a doctor in the audience and he came backstage to examine him. The ankle bone was fractured. The doctor advised him to go to the hospital immediately, but Houdini was unwilling to disappoint the audience. He said that he would go after the show. The ankle was taped up and he limped back onstage, still in his swimming trunks. He announced to the cheering audience that if they would give him a moment to change into evening dress, then the show would go on. He continued the performance without skimping a trick. At the end he was given an ovation.

Later, at the hospital, the ankle was set and put in a cast. He was advised to cancel his performances, but he was not prepared to do this. That night he could not sleep for the pain and he passed the time fashioning a leg brace to get him through the week. On Sunday the show travelled to Montreal. On Monday, the 18th, it opened at the Princess Theatre. The ankle was very painful, but his concern was all for Bess. Although she was able to travel, she was still a very sick woman.

He gave himself no chance to rest. On Tuesday afternoon he honoured a commitment to lecture on spiritualist fraud at McGill University. Afterwards he was surrounded by enthusiastic students. One of them, Samuel J. Smiley, showed him a pencil sketch he had made of him during the lecture. Houdini thought it an excellent likeness and invited Smiley to come backstage during the week and do some additional studies.

On Friday, the 22nd, Smiley and a fellow student, Jack Price, came to Houdini's dressing room in the afternoon. He was sitting on a couch, sorting through his mail. Smiley began to sketch him. There was a knock on the door and another student entered. He had come to return a book Houdini had loaned him. He was a strange looking student, well over six feet tall with thinning hair. His name was J. Gordon Whitehead. He began questioning Houdini, asking him what he thought of the miracles in the Bible. Houdini, busy with his mail, answered vaguely. But Whitehead continued questioning him, asking if it was true that he could take the hardest punch in his stomach without harm. Houdini said that he could, provided he had warning to brace himself. Whitehead asked if he could take a few trial punches. Houdini, still preoccupied with his mail, began to get up from the couch. Before he had time to brace himself. Whitehead punched him in the stomach with all his strength. Houdini's face creased with pain. Whitehead struck him again three times; he seemed to have gone berserk. Smiley and Price pulled him away. Houdini assured them that he was all right and the three students left together.

His stomach was sore and before evening it began to pain. That night he went through the show in agony. The pain was so bad that he could not sleep, but he believed the trouble to be no more than muscular. The next day, Saturday, he struggled through the matinee and evening performances. After the show the company boarded the train for Detroit, where they were booked for a two week run. When the train started, the pain was so intense that he could hide it no longer. He told Bess about the blows to his stomach. Nurse Rosenblatt took his temperature and found it to be 102 degrees.

The train was scheduled to stop at London, Ontario, and from there a telegram was despatched to the show's advance man in Detroit, instructing him to have a doctor waiting. When Houdini arrived the doctor examined him. He diagnosed acute appendicitis and ordered an ambulance to be called immediately. But Houdini refused to go into hospital right away. The theatre was sold out and he would not disappoint the audience. What it cost him no one knew, but he performed as he had always performed.

After the show he changed out of his evening dress and went to his hotel. Bess begged him to go into hospital, but he still hesitated. She pleaded with him for more than two hours before his resistance went. At three o'clock on the morning of the 25th he was taken to Grace Hospital and in the afternoon a ruptured appendix was removed. But the poison had seeped through his bloodstream for three days, peritonitis was far advanced and the doctors reckoned that he could not live for more than twelve hours. When Bess heard this, her own precarious health failed her and she suffered a relapse. She was given a room in the hospital and Nurse Rosenblatt attended her.

His brothers and sister, Dash, Nat and Gladys, arrived from New York. Leopold, still unforgiven by the family, was not asked to be present at his brother's death bed. Houdini told all his visitors that he would soon be on his feet. He knew what his chances were, but he had decided on one final battle with Death. For seven days he fought and fought and fought, confounding the doctors' prognosis. But on Sunday morning he had no strength left and he told Dash that he was tired of fighting. Nurse Rosenblatt brought Bess to him for her daily visit. He grasped Bess's hand and held it to his heart. He made her repeat over to him their solemn pact that whoever died first would try to come back. He told her that although his mother had never come to him, she herself must be prepared. He made her repeat the words of their agreed message, ROSABELLE followed by the code words for BELIEVE. He told her that when she heard these words she would know that it was he who was speaking; but only if she heard them in that formation, for he would never come back otherwise.

Bess, sick as she was, sat by his side all that day. Midnight came and went, still she sat. Then she sensed something was happening to him. She leaned over and put her arms around him. He could not speak, but his eyes were on her face, clear and questioning. Then he closed them and was dead. The time was 1.26 a.m. The date was 31 October, Hallowe'en, the night when all the spirits are abroad on earth.

*

His premonition of his death had come true and so did his prediction about the bronze coffin. During his illness all the equipment for the show had been crated and sent to New York, but by an oversight the coffin remained in Detroit. Now his body was placed in it. He had left a sealed letter containing instructions for his burial. He was laid beside his mother and his head rested on a black bag containing all the letters she had ever written to him. At the graveside Rabbi Bernard Drachman said that Houdini had possessed a wondrous power which he never understood and never revealed in life. Francis Werner, past President of the Society of American Magicians, broke a magic wand in half over the coffin and said that God had touched Houdini with a wondrous gift and he had made use of it. Those who maintained that Houdini had possessed psychic power read into these words a confirmation of their belief. Doyle asked the question, What could that power be except the power of the medium?

The ordinary people of Europe and America mourned the death of Houdini, but they knew of his promise to come back. It was said that in the manner of his return he would demonstrate immortality so vividly that no one would ever be able to disbelieve again and all the world would be converted. In the quiet of their home, Bess waited for him to return. Every Sunday, at the hour his soul left his body, she spent alone in prayer. On

the wall beside her was a large photograph of him, and in front
of this a light burned. She re-read the letters, the loving notes,
he had written to her. In a last note written on his death bed,
he told her to remember that he had loved only two women in
his life, his mother and herself, and signed himself, Yours in
Life, Death and Ever After. He had made other pacts with his
friends, but she was certain that if he could come back he would
come to her.

She attended seances at the same hour. Sometimes the mediums
said that he had come, that he was with them in the room. They
passed on messages, they spoke in his voice, but none of them
could give the code message that would establish beyond doubt
that he was truly present. From all over the country, from all
parts of the world, mediums claimed that he had come back,
weeping bitterly, repentant, begging forgiveness for his persecu-
tion of the spiritualist movement. But to none of them had he
given the message. The mediums said that as a punishment he
was not being allowed to come back on his own terms. Bess
offered ten thousand dollars to any medium who could give her
the proof she sought. Messages continued to pour in, some so
persuasive and evidential as to make her catch her breath, but
she repudiated them all. Unless the code message came through
she would not believe.

Fifteen months went by. The number of messages dwindled,
but it was a poor week if newspapers could not report at least
one from Houdini. Bess's hope was dying. Then, on 8 February
1928, an extraordinary incident occurred. A medium named
Arthur Ford was holding a seance with a group of friends. Ford
was pastor of the First Spiritualist Church of Manhattan. He
was young and handsome, with the manners of a Southern
gentleman. His spirit guide was David Fletcher, another young
man, whose voice like his own was soft and slightly lisping.

During the seance Ford went into a trance and through him
Fletcher announced that he had with him a woman he had not
seen before. The woman said that she was the mother of Houdini
and that for many years her son had waited for one word from
her. He had always said that if he could get this word he would

believe. Conditions had developed in her family which made it necessary for her to get the word through before he could give his wife the code he had arranged with her. If her family acted upon her word, he would be free and able to speak for himself. Her word was FORGIVE. She had tried on innumerable occasions to say it to him. Now he was with her and she was able to get through. She asked that the word be taken to Bess, who would declare it to be true.

There the message ended and Ford came out of his trance. He always said that he knew nothing of what occurred during a trance. He only learned this after a seance when he read the record which was kept by a member of the group. When he read the message from Houdini's mother, he thought it imperative that Bess should know. A copy was delivered to her the following day. It can be imagined with what astonishment she read it. She wrote to Ford saying that this was the first message she had received among thousands which had the appearance of truth. She also made a public statement that this was the sole communication that contained a key word known only to Houdini and herself.

The door between Bess and Houdini had opened. Now that the message from his mother had been delivered he was, according to her, free to send his own message to Bess. To keep this door open, Ford, together with a group of friends, began a series of seances. For nine months nothing happened. Then, in November, the first word of the code message came through. Spelling out the entire message took eight separate sittings, covering a period of two and a half months. The words came one at a time and David Fletcher, the spirit guide, was not certain of their correct sequence. Then one night he declared that the first word was ROSABELLE. He said that there were also some French words, an additional message, but that he would work on the main one first. At a sitting on 5 January 1929 he announced that he had the correct sequence. A man was telling him that it had taken him three months working out the confusion in order to get the words through and at no time had he been able to do anything without his mother's help. The words were

ROSABELLE ANSWER TELL PRAY ANSWER LOOK TELL
ANSWER ANSWER TELL. These words were to be taken to
the man's wife. She must sit with Ford, when he would repeat
the words to her. He would not reveal their meaning until then.

When the code words were handed to Bess, she was lying on
a couch with her head wrapped in bandages. A few days previously, ill with influenza, she had fainted and fallen down a
flight of stairs. She read the message and asked Ford to come to
the house the next day.

On 8 January she sat with Ford. The rest of the group was
made up of his friends and hers. They gathered round the couch
on which she lay. The seance began shortly after mid-day. Ford
went into a trance and Fletcher came through saying that the
man was here and wanted to say hello to Bess. The man wanted
to repeat the message and finish it for her. He said the code was
the one they used to use in their mind reading act. Fletcher
repeated the ten words and said that the man wanted her to say
whether they were correct or not. Bess said that they were correct.

Fletcher said that the man was smiling. He wanted her to take
off her wedding ring and tell the group what ROSABELLE
meant. Bess drew the ring from her finger. It was an extra wide
gold band and on the inside were engraved the words of the
song. She began to sing in a small voice:

> Rosabelle, sweet Rosabelle,
> I love you more than I can tell;
> O'er me you cast a spell,
> I love you, my Rosabelle.

Her voice broke and she could sing no more. Fletcher said that
there was something the man wanted to tell her, something that
no one but she knew. He said that the man was smiling again
and drawing curtains together in a certain manner. The man was
asking what she said next. Bess was quietly crying. '*Je tire le
rideau comme ça!* she whispered. 'I draw the curtains so!' the
phrase he had rehearsed with her over and over again, when they
had first played in Paris. She had said it gaily, during Metamorphosis, when she closed the curtains of the cabinet to hide the
trunk.

Houdini was now speaking to her directly, telling her that the message he wanted to send back to her was ROSABELLE BELIEVE. Fletcher asked her if this was correct and Bess said yes.

Houdini spoke again. He told her to tell the whole world that Houdini still lived and would prove it a thousand times or more. He was sorry that he had resorted to tricks to prove spirit communication untrue. She was to tell those who had lost faith because of his mistake to lay hold again of hope and to live with the knowledge that life was continuous. That, he said, was his message to the world.

*

And the world soon heard it. The news broke in time for the afternoon papers and was flashed around the globe. Houdini had come back! He still lived! Afterlife and spirit communication had been proved beyond doubt! The spiritualists rejoiced. He that was lost had been found. He that was dead had been restored to life. A new chapter was beginning for the human race. What glories and mysteries might not be revealed with such a powerful spirit in touch with the world! Margery, who had suffered such humiliation at his hands, issued a dignified and compassionate statement, saying she was glad that in death he had furnished the world with evidence which refuted the theories he had defended in life. Doyle heard the news and thanked God for it.

Joe Rinn also heard the news and to him it didn't sound at all like his old friend, especially the message to the world. He regarded the whole affair as the spook trick to end all spook tricks, a trick that must be exposed at once, or Houdini's great crusade would be discredited and the spiritualists have the final victory over him. Bess was convinced of the truth of Ford's seances, so Rinn and other friends of Houdini reminded her of certain things, which in her emotional state she had forgotten. Ford's message from Houdini's mother had included the evidential word FORGIVE, but the Brooklyn *Eagle* of 13 March 1927, a year before Ford's seance, had quoted Bess as saying that any authentic communication from Houdini's mother would have to include that word. Ford could have read this. She was also reminded that the code words used had been printed in Harold Kellock's biography of Houdini, in which she had collaborated, and which had been published the previous year. Moreover, Nurse Rosenblatt had usually been present when she visited Houdini's room during his final illness. The nurse could have overheard him asking her to repeat the formation of the code words and their meaning. This information could have been passed to Ford. Bess admitted that she had not thought of any of these things. But then at the time of the seance she was a sick woman, physically incapacitated, emotionally run down. No wonder she was confused.

Suddenly everyone was confused. On 10 January, two days after the seance, the New York *Graphic* published the following startling disclosures. The Houdini message was a hoax. One of their reporters had been in possession of the code words twenty-four hours before the seance. Ford, in the hearing of witnesses, had admitted being a close friend of Bess's for some time. Indeed he and Bess were planning a joint lecture tour, which he was financing and for which she had supplied the code as her part of the deal.

Bess denied this strenuously, saying that she had never betrayed Houdini's trust. She did admit, however, that she had known Ford prior to the seance. Perhaps during their intimate talks together he had persuaded her to confide much more than the French phrase and the inscription on the inside of her wedding ring. When she fully recovered from her illness, she repudiated Ford's message as she had repudiated all previous ones.

The years went by and the number of messages dwindled. Each year she held a seance on the anniversary of Houdini's death. She held the last seance on 31 October 1936, the tenth anniversary. After this she made no further attempts to get in touch with him. She died on 11 February 1943. To the end of her life she maintained that she had never received a communication from Houdini. Bess died, but the seances went on. Magicians and spiritualists, all wanted to get in touch with him. The code words could no longer be regarded as proof and mediums claimed that

Houdini had discarded these and came through in other ways.

The seances still go on and occasionally some story of a Houdini message is reported in the press, with an explanation for the younger generation of his vow to do all in his power to return. The mediums claim that he does come back, especially to those who are in sympathy with him. This led the present writer to consider attending a seance. He has spent the past three years in the company of Houdini and has come to love and admire him. But although he believes in life after death he cannot bring himself to believe in spirit communication, and he honours Houdini too much to engage in what he would regard as no more than a charade. And yet, and yet . . . who knows? Perhaps Houdini is out there, still seeking a way of returning. If there is a gate between the two worlds, then the courageous, restless, questioning spirit that mastered every lock on earth may well be the one to open it.

A Note on the Explanations of Houdini's Magic and Escapes

In *A Magician Among the Spirits* Houdini stated: 'I may elect to divulge my secrets. But I hope to carry these secrets to the grave as they are of no material benefit to mankind, and if they should be used by dishonest persons they might become a serious detriment.'

From this and other statements made by Houdini the belief arose that his secrets had died with him. But this was not so. Within a few years of his death, many of them had been revealed. They were made known by Walter B. Gibson, a writer on magic and kindred subjects. He was a close friend of Houdini and had 'ghosted' some of his writings. At the time of Houdini's death Gibson was preparing three volumes on simple magic, which were to appear under Houdini's name. These were to be the fore-runners of more ambitious titles. In his Introduction to *Houdini on Magic,* Gibson stated that after Houdini's death Bernard M. L. Ernst, Houdini's attorney, furnished him with 'a large amount of material that Houdini had laid away through the years, specifically stating that some day it should be published'. It was from this material that he completed the two volumes which appeared as *Houdini's Escapes* and *Houdini's Magic.*

Houdini himself had explained some of his methods during his own lifetime. He had done so whenever these had already become known or he had replaced them with something better. This made sense, as it lessened the value of such methods when they were appropriated by his rivals. Yet, surprisingly, he also revealed some of his secrets while he was still using them in his own act. For example, he disclosed some of his handcuff methods while continuing to perform the Challenge Handcuff Escape. Gibson's explanation of this is intriguing: 'Houdini's purpose was twofold. He wanted to establish himself as the pioneer of the Challenge Act and at the same time worry his imitators by giving away the more common devices upon which they depended. Frequently, along with crediting himself with certain inventions, Houdini disclaimed inferior methods as though he would never have stooped to their use. So even Houdini's exposures carry the implication that his own work approached the supernatural.'

Houdini's usual method of revealing his secrets was through articles published in his own *Conjurers' Monthly Magazine*. Some of these were later reprinted in book form under the title *Handcuff Secrets* and *Magical Rope Ties and Escapes*. Gibson, together with Morris N. Young, compiled a collection of Houdini's writings on magic taken from these two books, from other articles in the *Conjurers' Monthly Magazine,* and from the material Gibson had used in compiling his two earlier volumes. This book was published under the title *Houdini on Magic*.

A book explaining Houdini's methods was written by J. C. Cannell, a British journalist and amateur magician. Although he was a friend of Houdini, he did not have access to his private records and so he does not write with the same authority as Gibson. He gives no source for his explanations, but there is reason to believe that it was Will Goldston, British magician and confidant of Houdini. Cannell's explanations, which are substantially the same as those edited by Gibson, were published under the title *The Secrets of Houdini*.

Of the biographies, *Houdini,* by Harold Kellock, reveals none of his secrets, save one—the explanation of the map on the slate which mystified Theodore Roosevelt. William Lindsay Gresham incorporated the work of Gibson and Cannell into his book *Houdini: The Man Who Walked Through Walls*. In addition to these sources, Gresham acknowledged the help of The Amazing Randi (James Randall Zwinge), a Canadian magician, who carried on the Houdini tradition of escapes. The Amazing Randi duplicated some of Houdini's feats and in one case surpassed

him, when, in London, in November 1958, he remained submerged inside a coffin for two hours and three minutes, approxi-
mately thirty-three minutes longer than Houdini. Milbourne
Christopher, in *Houdini: The Untold Story*, adheres strictly to
the magician's code of secrecy and gives no explanations.

With so much documentation one would think that by now
the mystery of Houdini had been finally solved. But this is not
the case. There are still many people who do not accept these
explanations. They find them too remarkable and ingenious.
Indeed, if anything, the explanations have reinforced the conviction of those who believe Houdini to have had supernatural
powers. Let Bess Houdini have the last word. Writing to Sir
Arthur Conan Doyle, on 16 December 1926, she stated: 'He
buried no secrets. Every conjurer knows how his tricks were done
—with the exception of just where or how the various traps or
mechanisms were hidden ... it was Houdini himself that was
the secret.'

Annotated Bibliography

BIRD, J. MALCOLM. *'Margery' the medium*. John Hamilton, 1925.
A complete record of the Margery seances up to 1925. The author was an associate editor of *Scientific American* and secretary to its investigating committee into psychic phenomena. The book is persuasively written and seemingly detacned, but it is really extremely partisan. Mis-statements are made and vital facts warped in favour of Margery. During the investigation Houdini denounced the author as her confederate. The book contains a highly critical and basically inaccurate account of Houdini's role in the investigation.

BOSTON, GEORGE L. and PARRISH, ROBERT. *Inside magic*. New York, The Beechhurst Press, 1947.
For many years George L. Boston was a magician's chief assistant and he stresses the importance of this position. He believes that it is essential for a magician to have his chief assistant near him at all times. He maintains that this view is borne out by the circumstances of Houdini's death. Had James Collins been present in the dressing room on that occasion he would never have allowed Houdini to be punched in the abdomen while unprepared. The book gives insights into Houdini's routines based on the author's conversations with Collins.

CANNELL, J. C. *The secrets of Houdini*. Hutchinson & Co., 1931.

See under 'A note on the explanations of Houdini's magic and escapes'.

CARR, JOHN DICKSON. *The life of Sir Arthur Conan Doyle.* John Murray, 1949.
A highly-considered work, which surprisingly makes no mention of Houdini.

CHARNLEY, DAVID H. *Magic: the great illusions revealed and explained.* Robert Hale & Co., 1976.
Based on *Magic* by Albert A. Hopkins, first published in 1897, this book gives detailed explanations of the classic illusions, levitation, disappearance, decapitation, etc. It is not generally realised that by the end of the nineteenth century almost every principle of optics, mechanics, sound, and electricity had been applied to stage illusions and that twentieth century illusions are based mainly on the same principles.

CHRISTOPHER, MILBOURNE. *Houdini: the untold story.* Cassell, 1969.
The author is a giant figure in the world of magic today. He is not only a top-ranking performer but also an authority on the history of magic and on Houdini in particular. Of all Houdini biographies this is the most detailed and accurate, but there is little attempt to assess the wider implications of his career and no insights into his psychology. While full accounts are given of Houdini's repertoire, the author, as a practising magician, adheres strictly to the magicians' code of secrecy and gives no explanations.
—— *The illustrated history of magic.* Robert Hale & Co., 1975.
A comprehensive and scholarly work. It is particularly strong on the development of stage magic from the eighteenth century onwards. The history is recounted mainly through biographical studies of the great magicians.

DOCTOROW, E. L. *Ragtime.* Macmillan, 1976.
A novel, but is included here because so little of any literary

value has been written about Houdini. He appears at intervals throughout the story, and while the facts of his life have been distorted, no other book so brilliantly evokes him.

DOYLE, SIR ARTHUR CONAN. *The edge of the unknown.* John Murray, 1930.

Contains a long essay entitled 'The riddle of Houdini', in which Doyle puts forward his case that Houdini had supernatural powers and argues it forcibly.

—— *Memories and adventures.* Hodder and Stoughton, 1924.

In Chapter XXXII, 'The psychic quest', he bears witness to the truth of spiritualism. He writes convincingly and movingly, revealing the cast of his mind and his child-like faith.

—— *Our American adventure.* Hodder and Stoughton, 1923. *Our second American adventure.* Hodder and Stoughton, 1924.

Recounts the story of his two lecture tours in America and his encounters there with Houdini. It is worth noting that Doyle considered these rather trite books, together with *The Wanderings of a Spiritualist,* which deals with his lecture tour of Australia, as a trilogy to be viewed in the same light as the *Acts of the Apostles.* Writing to Houdini, he states: '. . . if this mission of mine has any appreciable effect in altering the religious opinion of the world, then the time will come when the account of my travels may be very interesting and even valuable to those who follow me'.

DUNNINGER, JOSEPH. *Houdini's spirit exposés.* Edited by Joseph H. Kraus. New York, Experimenter Publishing Co., 1928.

The author was a celebrated mentalist and friend of Houdini. After Houdini's death, Dunninger acquired some of his files, among them records of investigations of fake mediums. The book is based on those records. It also contains Dunninger's own explanations of so-called psychic phenomena.

—— *Inside the medium's cabinet.* New York, David Kemp and Co., 1935.

As chairman of the *Science and Invention* Committee for Psychical Research, Dunninger carried on Houdini's work of exposing fake mediums. Among these was Nino Pecoraro, whom Houdini had worsted during the *Scientific American* investigation. The book is particularly valuable for the two chapters on the Houdini Messages received through the medium, Arthur Ford. Dunninger played a leading role in throwing doubt on the authenticity of the messages.

ERAS, VINCENT J. M. *Locks and keys throughout the ages.* Folkestone, Bailey Bros and Swinfen, 1974.
An authoritative history of the development of locks. These are so many and various that the reader is able to appreciate more fully the extent of Houdini's achievement in mastering them.

ERNST, BERNARD M. L. and CARRINGTON, HEREWARD (EDITORS). *Houdini and Conan Doyle: the story of a strange friendship.* New York, Albert and Charles Boni Inc., 1932.
Based on the letters that passed between the two men, this is a key work in the study of Houdini. But it has to be used with care. Many of the letters have been placed out of sequence; others have been chopped up and the pieces scattered throughout several chapters. The editors justifiably do this to make their points, but it does not make matters easy for researchers who do not have access to the original material. The present writer resolved the difficulty by transcribing the letters, piecing the fragments together to form as complete a letter as possible, and arranging the whole chronologically. This enabled him to follow the development of the relationship between Houdini and Doyle without the views of the editors intruding at every step. He also found that some of the excerpts from the letters had been wrongly dated.

FAST, FRANCIS R. *The Houdini messages.* New York, Privately printed by the author. n.d. (c.1929)
The author was a confirmed spiritualist and close friend of the medium, Arthur Ford. He was present at the series of seances conducted by Ford, and took down the messages from Houdini and his mother that came through David Fletcher, Ford's spirit guide. He had no doubt at all of their authenticity.

FORD, ARTHUR and BRO, MARGUERITE HARMON. *Nothing so strange.* New York, Harper & Brothers, 1958.
Ford's own story of his career as a medium. It contains a detailed account of the seances at which messages from Houdini and his mother were received. At first Houdini's wife believed these to be genuine, but later repudiated them. Ford's account is persuasive, as would be expected from a man whom Joe Rinn described as the most intelligent of American mediums.

GIBSON, WALTER B. *Houdini's escapes.* New York, Harcourt, Brace & Co., 1930.
See under 'A note on the explanations of Houdini's magic and escapes'.
—— *Houdini's magic.* New York, Harcourt, Brace & Co., 1932.
See under 'A note on the explanations of Houdini's magic and escapes'.
—— *The original Houdini scrapbook.* Oak Tree Press, 1977.
A marvellous compilation of printed ephemera relating to Houdini. Useful to the researcher because of the amount of primary source material included.

GILBERT, DOUGLAS. *American vaudeville: its life and times.* New York, Whittlesey House, 1940.
A splendid account of the entertainment form of which Houdini was one of the greatest stars. It includes sections on the beer halls and dime museums in which he made his earliest appearances. Spanning as it does the half-century between 1880 and 1930, the book covers the entire background of his vaudeville career.

GRESHAM, WILLIAM LINDSAY. *Houdini: the man who walked through walls.* Victor Gollancz, 1960.
A biography of Houdini written by a man who is thoroughly at home in the world of vaudeville and carnival midways. Un-

fortunately this makes him see Houdini solely as a showbiz character and to impute almost all his motives to showmanship. The book is not so detailed as Milbourne Christopher's biography, but it is better written, although the author is, at times, inclined to be somewhat breezy. This was the first biography to incorporate explanations of Houdini's tricks. (*See also* 'A note on the explanations of Houdini's magic and escapes')

HALL, TREVOR H. *Sherlock Holmes and his creator.* Duckworth, 1978.
  Contains a scholarly essay entitled 'Conan Doyle and spiritualism', which succeeds in giving a balanced view of Doyle's involvement with the subject.

HARMON, JIM and GLUT, DONALD F. *The great movie serials: their sound and fury.* Woburn Press, 1973.
  Houdini's career in the movie industry is not considered important enough to merit more than the briefest reference in serious histories of the subject. Some do not mention him at all. This book gives a synopsis of the plot of his silent serial 'The Master Mystery'.

HENNING, DOUG and REYNOLDS, CHARLES. *Houdini: his legend and his magic.* New York, Times Books, 1977.
  Doug Henning is an American magician who appears to regard himself as the re-incarnation of Houdini. His silhouetted profile is given equal prominence on the title page. The book is included here for the useful essay by Charles Reynolds, in which he sifts the truth of Houdini's life from the legends.

HIGHAM, CHARLES. *The Adventures of Conan Doyle: the life of the creator of Sherlock Holmes.* Hamish Hamilton, 1976.
  Contains a brief and accurate account of Doyle's relationship with Houdini.

HOUDINI
Only the more substantial works of Houdini are listed here. He

published many pamphlets and was a prolific contributor to periodicals. A definitive bibliography of all his writings, compiled by
Manuel Weltman, was published in *Genii*, the monthly conjurers'
periodical, in October, November, December 1967, and January
1968.

—— *Handcuff secrets.* George Routledge & Sons 1910.
See under 'A note on the explanations of Houdini's magic
and escapes'.

—— *Houdini on magic.* Edited by Walter B. Gibson and
Morris N. Young. New York, Dover Publications, 1953.
See under 'A note on the explanations of Houdini's magic
and escapes'.

—— *Magical rope ties and escapes.* Will Goldston, 1921.
See under 'A note on the explanations of Houdini's magic
and escapes'.

—— *A magician among the spirits.* New York, Harper &
Brothers, 1924.

Houdini's account of the development of spiritualism shows it
to be a history of fraud from the Fox sisters onwards. Although
weakened by some inaccurate statements, which the spiritualists
were able to turn against him, the book was a devastating attack
on their movement and made a great impact on the public. It
contains a full account of the Atlantic City seance conducted by
Lady Doyle.

—— *Miracle mongers and their methods.* New York, E. P.
Dutton & Co., 1921.

An exposé of the methods of fire eaters, sword swallowers,
gravity resisters, and other sideshow acts, many of which he had
personally studied when he played the dime museums and
carnival midways.

—— *The right way to do wrong.* Boston, Massachusetts, Published by Houdini, 1906.

An exposé of the methods of criminals—burglars, pickpockets,
confidence men, etc. Written during his jail-breaking phase, it
was partly a public relations exercise to show that he was firmly
on the side of law and order. It has been said that the crooks
themselves bought up most of the copies to prevent their methods

from becoming too widely known, and that this accounts for the rarity of the booklet today.

—— *The unmasking of Robert-Houdin.* New York, The Publisher Printing Co., 1908.

Yet another exposé, this time of his erstwhile hero. Not always accurate, as defenders of Robert-Houdin have pointed out. (*See also* Sardina, Maurice. 'Where Houdini was wrong') The claims of Robert-Houdin had never been seriously considered by magic scholars, and so Houdini's passionate denunciation seemed somewhat extreme. But the book does express his bitter disappointment in discovering that the hero, on whom he had based his name, should be a man who regarded truth so lightly, filching the tricks of his predecessors and passing them off as his own inventions.

INGLIS, BRIAN. *Natural and supernatural: a history of the paranormal from earliest times to 1914.* Hodder and Stoughton 1977.

The author's method is an original one. He deals not so much with the psychology of the practitioners of the paranormal and supernatural as with that of their detractors, both scientific and religious. The book is of particular interest here when he applies his method to the great spiritualist mediums from the Fox sisters onward. Throughout he brings forward much evidence to show that there have been a large number of paranormal and supernatural happenings that cannot be rejected as fraud.

KELLOCK, HAROLD. *Houdini: his life-story,* by Harold Kellock from the recollections and documents of Beatrice Houdini. New York, Harcourt, Brace & Co., 1928.

The first biography of Houdini. It is based on his scrapbooks, diaries, and his wife's reminiscences. These reminiscences tend to be sentimental, emphasising the great love they had for one another. The book is important for the extensive quotations from Houdini's private writings. (*See also* 'A note on the explanations of Houdini's magic and escapes')

A personal note: This is the book referred to in the Dedication.

LAHUE, KALTON C. *Bound and gagged: the story of the silent serials.* New York, A. S. Barnes and Co., 1968.
Gives a brief assessment of Houdini's serial 'The Master Mystery'.

McKENZIE, JAMES HEWAT. *Spirit intercourse: its theory and practice.* Simpkin, Marshall, Hamilton Kent and Co., 1916.
The author was head of the British College of Psychic Science, a body founded by his wife and himself. He discusses the role psychic forces play in human life, citing Houdini's ability to open locks as an example. He describes the occasion when he was a member of the committee onstage during a performance of the Torture Cell Escape. He was convinced that Houdini escaped by dematerialising himself. In *A magician among the spirits* Houdini refers to this as one of 'the most, if not the most, flagrant instances of mal-observation I have ever known'.

PRINCE, WALTER FRANKLIN. 'A review of the Margery case'. *American Journal of Psychology,* July 1926.
The author was a distinguished psychic investigator and a member of the *Scientific American* committee. This is an excellent analysis of the scientific attempts to investigate Margery. He considers how the investigation was hampered by the rules laid down by her husband, and by spiritualists in general, concerning 'psychic laws'. He questions the validity of these rules, which work against the discovery of fraud.

PROSKAUER, JULIEN J. *The dead do not talk.* New York, Harper & Brothers, 1946.
The author was a journalist and a magician. He was a friend of Houdini, who supplied him with information about the methods of fake mediums. That information is vividly conveyed in this book. The author acknowledged Houdini as the greatest 'ghost breaker' of all time and was determined to follow in his footsteps. The book takes up where 'Spook crooks' leaves off. *(See below)*
—— *Spook crooks.* Selwyn & Blount, n.d. (c.1932)

Case histories of the victims of astrologers, mediums, and fortune tellers, together with details of fraudulent techniques. The author had access to Houdini's private records. This is stated in the Introduction, but it is not clear from the text to what extent he used them or to which cases they refer. The author had strong feelings on the subject and the book is passionately written. Houdini would have been proud to have written both this and the title above.

—— *The revelations of a spirit medium, or spiritualistic mysteries exposed. A detailed explanation of the methods used by fraudulent mediums.* St Paul, Minnesota, Farrington & Co., 1891.

This book had a great influence on Houdini. He read it when he was seventeen years old and turning over in his mind the idea of becoming a professional magician. Until reading it he had not the slightest knowledge of the fact that a person while securely bound with ropes could release himself and get back into his bonds. The book explained how the trick was done.

RINN, JOSEPH FRANCIS. *Searchlight on psychical research.* Rider & Co., 1954.

An important work in the study of Houdini written by his lifelong friend. Up to 1923 Rinn led the field in the investigation of fake mediums in America. Houdini's later work in exposing spook crooks owed much to techniques perfected by Rinn, who makes this very clear in the book. Indeed it would seem that Houdini was constantly consulting him, and the reader must make allowance for the vanity of a man whose achievements have been eclipsed by those of his friend. For all that it is an affectionate book, giving much first-hand information about Houdini at different stages of his life.

ROBERT-HOUDIN, JEAN EUGENE. *Memoirs of Robert-Houdin.* Translated from the French by Lascelles Wraxall. With a new introduction and notes by Milbourne Christopher. New York, Dover Publications, 1964.

The book that decided the course of Houdini's life. He read it when he was seventeen years old and it resolved all his doubts about becoming a professional magician. The book was first published in 1858 and quickly translated into most European languages. It is a romanticised autobiography worked up into a highly readable form with the aid of a Parisian journalist. The book is as appealing today as when it was first written. It is not hard to understand the effect it had on the young Houdini.

SARDINA, MAURICE. *Where Houdini was wrong.* Translated and edited with notes by Victor Farelli. Magic Wand, 1950.

The author defends the integrity of Robert-Houdin against Houdini's accusations. (*See also* Houdini, 'The unmasking of Robert-Houdin')

UNITED STATES. HOUSE OF REPRESENTATIVES. *Fortune telling.* Hearings before the Subcommittee on Judiciary of the Committee on the District of Columbia, Sixty-Ninth Congress, First Session on H. R. 8989 February 26; May 18, 20, 21, 1926. Washington, Government Printing Office, 1926.

Surely one of the most curious records in the archives of the Library of Congress. Houdini testifies against the spook crooks of Washington and publicly declares his love for his wife.

WILSON, EDMUND. 'A great magician'. *New Republic* Vol. LVI, 17 October 1928.

Written after reading Harold Kellock's biography of Houdini, Wilson assesses Houdini's 'unique position'. He suggests that by the time of his death Houdini had reached the limits of his capacity and exhausted the possibilities of his field.

—— 'Houdini'. *New Republic,* Vol. XLIII, 24 June 1925.

The first of two perceptive articles by a distinguished literary critic, himself an amateur magician. Wilson was among the first to recognise the significance of Houdini's achievement. He describes Houdini's performance in his final magic show and goes on to discuss his importance as an investigator of psychic phenomena. He suggests that Houdini has appeared at a crucial moment in the history of spiritualism and is destined to play a great role.

G

ZELLERS, PARKER, *Tony Pastor: dean of the vaudeville stage.*
Ypsilanti, Eastern Michigan University Press, 1971.
Tony Pastor was the most influential figure in the evolution
of vaudeville. He was also the first impresario to give Houdini
his chance of the big-time. Surprisingly no mention is made of
this, but the book does give a good account of the field in which
Houdini worked for so many years.

Acknowledgements

I owe a debt to Alan Snowden of the Magic Circle for the help and encouragement he has given me throughout the writing of this book. I am also grateful to Peter D. Blanchard, A. W. Lanman, Leonard Saunders, and Mac Wilson, all members of the Circle, for the interest they have taken. I thank Bill Larsen of the Magic Castle in Hollywood for sending so promptly the information I required, and Richard Fawkes for material on the Davenport brothers. And I thank my dear friend, Christopher Calthrop, not only for the research he undertook on my behalf in the United States but for many, many other things.

Index

Abbot, David P. (psychic investigator), tells J. Rinn of trumpet medium, 72

Alfonso XII, King of Spain, invites Herrmann the Great to palace, 6

American, New York, publishes Rinn's attack on Doyle, 124

Anderson, John Henry (magician), catches bullet in his teeth, 52–3

Argamasilla, Joaquin Maria ('The Man with the X-Ray Eyes'), exposed by H, 132

Balfour, Arthur James, 1st Earl of Balfour (statesman), experiments in thought transference, 146–8

Bamberg family (magicians), 52

Barnum, Phineas Taylor (showman), 12

Baruch, Bernard M. (financier), assists in H's thought transference experiments, 148–9

Beck, Martin (vaudeville booking agent), notices H, 36; reservations about H's showmanship, 37; advises H, 37, 50–1, 57

Beer halls, 15

Bey, Rahman ('Egyptian Miracle Worker'), buried alive, 157–8

Bird, J. Malcolm (secretary to *Scientific American* committee), persuades Margery to appear before committee, 135–6; forms sub-committee to investigate Margery, 136; friendship with Crandons, 136–7; role in seances, 136–7, 138, 139; convinced Margery genuine, 137; excluded from seances, 140; resigns as secretary, 142; denounced by H, 145; record of Margery seances, 173

Blake, Mrs (medium), baffles D. P. Abbott, 72

Bloom, Solomon (Representative, New York state), introduces anti-fortune telling bill, 153

Boston, George L. (magician's assistant), on H's death, 173

Burton, Sir Richard Francis (explorer and orientalist), rejects Maskelyne's duplication of Davenport's phenomena, 74

Cannell, J. C. (journalist), explanations of H's magic and escapes, 171

Carrington, Hereward (psychic investigator), investigates E. Palladino, 72; becomes member *Scientific American* committee, 122; investigates Margery, 136; convinced Margery genuine, 137; withdraws from Margery seances, 140; denounced by H, 145; sponsors Rahman Bey, 157–8

Cirnoc, P. H. (handcuff escape performer), encounter with H, 41–2

Coates, Jane B. (medium), believes H to be a mystic, 155

Collins, James (H's assistant), works with H on Torture Cell, 83; assists H in Torture Cell Escape, 87–8, 160; rescues H, 99; visits A. Martin, 125; devises cabinet to hold Margery, 140; reinforces cabinet, 142; assists H in underwater burial, 159; possible prevention of H's death, 173

Comstock, Daniel Fisk (member *Scientific American* committee), 122; investigates Margery, 136, 137, 140, 141; verdict on Margery, 144

Conjurer's Monthly Magazine, started by H, 70–1

Coolidge, John Calvin (President,

Raymund FitzSimons is an authority on nineteenth-century literature and theater, subjects on which he has written and lectured for many years. He has made a special study of showmen and showmanship. He has also written plays and features for radio and television.

His interest in Houdini has been lifelong. Although not a practicing magician, he is an associate member of the Magic Circle, elected for his interest in the literature of magic.

He is married and has four teen-age children, and lives in a yellow brick Victorian house in the picturesque village of Wetheral, in Cumbria, England.